AGNES SANFORD:

"The collection of books that we call the Bible is the drama of God and man and of the earth whereupon God established man and to whom He gave dominion over it.... The bits and glimpses that I will pick out in this book and endeavor to illumine with common sense will be those bits that show the interweaving of the three: God and Man and Earth."

"If we can look at the very thing that plagued us, and believe that it can be turned into a source of healing, then it will be a tool of power, a stepping-stone instead of a stumbling block."

THE HEALING POWER OF THE BIBLE

Agnes Sanford

PILLAR BOOKS NEW YORK

To those who wonder and to those who
question, this book is dedicated.

THE HEALING POWER OF THE BIBLE
A PILLAR BOOK

Published by arrangement with J. B. Lippincott Company

Pillar Books edition published August 1976

ISBN: 0-89129-192-X

Printed in the United States of America

PILLAR BOOKS
Pyramid Publications
(Harcourt Brace Jovanovich, Inc.)
757 Third Avene, New York, New York 10017, U.S.A.

Contents

✳

Foreword

✳

For centuries the Bible has been a bulwark of strength all over the world: the best-seller of all best-sellers of all times.

My three-year-old grandson once showed me joyfully a children's Bible. "I've got a book about God!" he said, his eyes shining, and he added rather quaintly, "My father wrote it."

In his first statement, at any rate, the child was right. The Bible is a book about God. That is why power seems to flow out of it. There is more in the Bible than mere information. A numinous quality, an emanation of that kind of spiritual energy that we call faith, seems to connect with the very book itself. Moreover I believe that this power is increased by the prayers and love of all who have read the Bible through the centuries.

For myself, I still prefer the King James Version to more modern translations. The quaintness of the style amuses me, and the ambiguous quality of some of the statements piques my curiosity so that I try to solve those enigmas. Moreover, having memorized this Bible daily from early childhood (not always of my own volition), I have it still there deep in the mind, an abiding foundation of faith. Therefore, even the cadence of this ancient version of the Bible speaks to some part of me beyond and above the mind. However, I am grateful for modern translations and for the new light that they shed on the old text.

As one grows toward maturity, disturbing doubts nevertheless cast shadows upon this "book about God."

How can He have made the world in six days, when the evidence of science suggests a growing period of billions of years? How can a flood have covered the whole earth? How could Elijah go up to heaven in a chariot of fire? Did Jesus really turn water into wine, and feed five thousand people with five loaves of bread?

The rationalist of the present day says No: these things are only ancient myths. But many of us cannot be content with this dismissal of the Holy Book. For if these stories of the Bible are not true, how can we believe in the miraculous birth of Jesus Christ, the Son of God? And if we do not believe, how can we sing of Jesus at Christmastime without sorrow filling our hearts? To many adults, Christmas has become a time of struggle against an inner heaviness, rather than a time of joy, but we do not let ourselves understand why this change has taken place within us. We close our minds to our own quite reasonable wonderings.

Our doubts are quite reasonable, and they are not insoluble. We find our answers not in evading doubts but in seriously looking for answers to them.

Where then shall we look? First of all, I believe we should learn as much as we can of the sciences that concern the universe. Science is the honest attempt of honest men to arrive at truth.

Second (rather, at the same time, for the two belong together), we should look again at the Bible, giving its ancient manuscripts the same respect and thoughtful consideration that we give to other ancient manuscripts, endeavoring to see how science and the Bible fit together, and how the one helps us to understand the other.

I am not a scientist, but only an ordinary person who tries to understand truth wherever I see it. My bits of information about the world around me I have gleaned from those wiser and more scholarly than I. The bit of understanding of the Bible that I have learned comes mostly from intensive study of that collection of books, Genesis to Revelation, chapter by chapter and verse by verse, helped by Bible dictionary, concordance, and commentaries.

The purpose of this book is not to study the whole Bible in depth. I am not using my insight as a microscope to probe into the text, or as a telescope to search the heavens and proclaim new theories and theologies. I use it only as a searchlight. A searchlight is a very little thing, really: only a single beam, trained to pick out spots here and there and to illumine them, leaving the main landscape in darkness.

It is my hope that in reading this book you will see how to use your own searchlight of common sense and inspired wondering, and that as you do so passages hitherto puzzling will be highlighted by truth. So I believe you will find released to you increasingly the healing and life-giving power of the Bible.

AGNES SANFORD
Monrovia, California

1
Creation

✳

In the beginning God created the earth and the world. "And God said, Let there be light: and there was light. . . . And the evening and the morning were the first day." (Gen. 1:3,5) And in the same chapter it is written that on the fourth day God created the sun and the moon. (Gen. 1:14-19) This always used to puzzle me. How could there be light on the first day when there was not as yet any sun to give light? How indeed could the evening and the morning be the first day when there was no earth to rotate around any sun, thus dividing twelve hours of light from twelve hours of darkness and making the morning?

My canvas was too small for the picture, that was all. I was thinking only of the planet earth, which in days of old we innocently assumed to be the world. But the "world" is the universe: a creation of such vastness, we now know, that the very thought of it staggers the imagination. In this illimitable emptiness of black space, amid these myriads of raging suns which are so far away that the speck of light we see from one of them might have begun its shining across space before this earth was even created—in this thunderous silence and this unbearable explosion of energy that is the universe, time as we know it does not exist. Time is relative. Scientists contemplating space flight have calculated that a flight taking 300,000 years of earth-time might affect the bodies of the spacemen as though it were only forty-five years.

The division of time, therefore, that men of old called the first "day" may have been in world-time (for

11

there was as yet no earth) an aeon or an epoch comprising billions of those small earth-time divisions later called years, each made up of 365 days of twenty-four hours.

The way of God's creation coincided exactly with the more advanced theories of creation taught in our sciences. In the beginning, astronomers declare, there was only the blackness of space: no movement, no light, no life. Then out of utter stillness there began to be a moving, a pulsing (the breath of God? the Word of God going forth?). And this moving and radiating energy was, and is, a kind of light, though the human eye cannot see it.

Science tells us that light is more than the glow of sun, moon, or electric bulb visible to the unaided eye. These are but the beginning of our ordinary light, made up of the seven primary colors of the rainbow. Beyond this light that we can see, there are the infra-red and the ultra-violet radiations of light that we cannot see with the unaided eye. Beyond these again, farther along the spectrum, are the radiations of X ray and of radium: light that we cannot see. A medical specialist in this field said to me, "I can see what it is, the light that heals. It is a radiation or vibration of light, farther along the spectrum, that is all. And it is the original source of life. It is pure creativity."

As the moving of this energy increased, the "light" caught fire, as it were, burst into flaming gases, and whirled them into those vast suns that we call stars, among which our sun is one of the least of suns. It is supposed by students of far time and illimitable space that the planets may have been bits of sun-life thrown off in the whirling, revolving journey around their mother-sun, tied to it by centrifugal force and cooling gradually in the deep, dark cold of that space through which they whirl.

Upon this whirling earth the light was divided from the darkness and there became night and day. No man could have lived upon this earth, nor could any living creature abide thereon, until in its cooling there was created the miracle of hydrogen and oxygen becoming air and separating the waters above (mist and cloud) from the waters below (seas and rivers). And the period of time in which this took place was called the second "day" of the Lord.

On the third "day" the dry land appeared and brought forth, most amazingly, grass and bushes and trees, the seed of each being within itself upon the earth: a spontaneous burst of life from the abounding and illimitable life of the creator, God expressing Himself in a new way in visible forms of beauty and fruitfulness.

So far the account of Genesis has tallied exactly with the findings of science. But now a bit of a puzzle arises, for we are told that on the fourth "day" the sun, moon, and stars were created. If, however, we give to this record the same respectful attention that we would give to any other ancient manuscript, the difficulty resolves itself. Not until this fourth "day," or aeon, of creation, could sun, moon or stars be seen, for the ever-arising mist covered the cooling earth.

It would have appeared, therefore, to any beings living upon the earth during the fourth "day" that the sun, moon, and stars were newly created, whereas a more exact word would be that they were finally brought forth into visibility by the clearing of the mists.

This seems to me perfectly clear and plain, yet those who read may find it puzzling. So let us use our imaginations together and tell ourselves a fairy story about this infant planet. It was born in fire and fierce heat, which heat and fire still burn within it, escaping here and there in volcanoes spouting fire upon the earth. The earth was flung out from the sun, according to the nebular theory of astronomy, into the deep-freeze of intersellar space. We have been in airplanes when the pilot has cheerfully told us that it was seventy degrees below zero outside. And here, mind you, the air was still tempered by the atmosphere of the earth. What would happen, then, when the bitter cold of space encountered the fire of the planet earth newborn from its mother sun? Would there not be a cooling, and would not the mingling of cold and heat produce fog, even as it does here in California when winds from the scorching desert blow into the cold ocean? This is not my fancy but is sober truth. The science of astronomy knows and tells us that the younger planet, Venus, is still surrounded by a mass of cloud fifty miles high.

Let us suppose that we now lived on Venus. We would see for about half the time a light by which we could walk. But we could not see through the cloud veil and perceive the sun, even as we on the earth cannot see the sun on a day of thick clouds. Therefore we could not know whence came that light. And if we had any feeling of the reality of a creator we could only say that He separated the light from the darkness. (Gen. 1:4) This darkness, during the time that we call night, would be an utter thick darkness, no moon visible through it and certainly no stars. One might notice that on some nights the darkness was not quite so impenetrable, but one could not know that there was a moon sending out its pale light far beyond the clouds.

As the cloud gradually thinned, one would some day see the sun and would be terrified and affrighted, and probably worship it as a god, which indeed some people do until this day. The day would come, however, when one would also see the moon, and even the stars. One might then conclude that the sun was not itself a god, but that upon this day God had created the sun to rule the day for the pleasure of man, and the moon and stars to delight and comfort him at night.

Man would see clearly that all these heavenly bodies revolved around the earth. Indeed for many centuries man did so think, and the first astronomer who taught that the earth revolved instead around the sun was persecuted as a dangerous heretic. Man could *see* the sun revolving around the earth. What could be a more dangerous heresy than to teach that the evidence of one's eyes did not always represent truth?

How amazing that the vision of man could reach back into these years when the earth was born with a veil of cloud, as a baby is sometimes born with a caul! How thrilling that man could even draw out of his deep mind, or out of God's omniscience, the picture of a time when the density of the cloud alone watered the earth, and when the phenomenon of rain had not yet come to the earth, even as the phenomenon of sunlight and shadow had not yet happened! (Gen. 2:5-6)

I am not the first person to tell a fairy story about this time before the beginning of our time. C. S. Lewis has told such a fairy story—a whole book of it—in his science fiction novel *Perelandra*. An earthman, Ransom, was mysteriously transported to that infant planet and met Eve of the planet—the first and only woman thereupon. He tried to explain to her the solar system as seen from the earth, even as our astronauts try to explain to us the view of the earth as seen from the moon. She listened in amazement, for of course she had never seen above the "roof," as she called the cloud-mass that enveloped her home planet.

"Beyond the roof it is all Deep Heaven, the high place," she said.

"How have you found all this out?" asked the earthman. "Your roof is so dense that your people cannot see through into Deep Heaven and look at the other worlds."

"Oh, I see it," she said, "I am older now. Your world has no roof. You look right out into the High Place and see the great dance with your own eyes. You live always in that terror and that delight, and what we must only believe you can behold."

So, truth in fantasy. For if a person lived on Venus now, he could see no stars or any sun, and could only wonder if told of the great dance of the stars and planets in their orbits.

On the fifth "day," animal life appeared, first of all in the ocean, just as science tell us. Then living creatures from the sea rose into the sky and learned to live in the air. So the Bible tells us, and so science tells us. And in the latest period of creation, living creatures, beginning in the ocean, spread upon the land and walked and lived upon it. So also the Bible and science tell us.

The last of these to be created, and the most involved and peculiar, was man. At this point science points to a "missing link," being unable to trace the creative process whereby man alone among all living creatures became conscious both of himself as a living entity, and of God as his creator.

"Let us make man in our image, after our likeness," said the plural creator, God in three persons, Father, Son, and Holy Spirit. "And let them have dominion" (Gen. 1:26), that is, let men carry on the work of creativity upon the earth.

In the creation of man the pattern of creativity was altered, and from the time man took over the dominion of the earth, the spontaneous creativity that some call evolution slowed down and ground to a halt. It had done its work. And that living creature that is the creation (Rom. 8:22-23) now awaited its fulfillment and its completion through the evolvement of the sons of God.

In Genesis 2 (vv. 4ff.) we find another ancient story of creation, nor is this in any way strange, for Moses gathered together the stories handed down for generations and ages before any man on earth could know how to write them. By the guidance and the power of God, Moses chose among old legends those wherein the Spirit of God had brought forth truth, and put them together. This second account contradicts nothing in the first story of creation, but adds to it fascinating facets of truth.

Man, then—the real essence and being of man— came directly from God in a new way of creation. We are told this new way in words of thunderous simplicity and of a depth that defies all comprehension: "And the Lord God formed man of the dust of the ground, and breathed into his nostrils the breath of life; and man became a living soul." (Gen. 2:7) The word "breath" *(ruach)* means "spirit." In a sense the whole created universe came from the Spirit of God, for the word of

God set life in motion. But this life of God which is in all the world is not sentient. Within a rock there is the high shining of the life of God, as modern photography brings forth, the light being actually visible on a very sensitive film even in a picture taken in darkness. But the rock does not *know* that the light of God is within it.

Into man, however, made in the image and likeness of God (Gen. 1:26), there was breathed the sentient and creative Spirit of God. This staggers the imagination, and yet if we are to receive to the full the power that is given us, we should try to grasp this truth: the Spirit and the power of God *abide in us*. We are not one person but two. In all of you who read, there is the one visible in the mirror, and there is the other one, existing at a different vibration of energy, who is not visible in the mirror. This other one, the spirit or the spiritual body, interpenetrates the body of flesh. You are living in two bodies at the same time. This one is mortal, and the other is immortal.

Come now! You know this! Have you Christian people never heard the statement that when you die you will go to heaven? Who will go to heaven? The one visible in the mirror? We trust that this also will be so in the fullness of the days of the Lord. (John 11:26) In the present "day" the body you see in the mirror will return to the dust of the earth from which God made it. But the other one of you will separate itself like a mist arising from the physical body, and will enter into a new way of life. How else would one "go to heaven"? Is it reasonable to think that God will make a different body out of nothing at all—or that He has your spiritual body put away in a box somewhere, and will at the moment of death take it out and shake away the wrinkles, and set it moving?

Is it not at least as sensible to think that your spiritual body lives *now*? And if it lives now, where is it? Why, in you, in and around your other body, its light permeating your physical body and emanating from your physical body and shining into the world around you. How do I know that this is true? Because I have seen this light, and many people have seen it, and so will you, if you will read on and meditate, and try what I suggest. And if you do not read and try, then you have no way of judging whether or not what I have written is true.

As I write this I am sitting in a tiny shack on a hill in New Hampshire in what I call my upper field. I am looking through the silent beauty of pine boughs, rifts of sun lighting them with a soft blue light. Faintly beyond them I see far hills. If someone were to say to me, "There is a lake below those hills," I would be stupid indeed if I were to say, "I cannot believe it." There is one sure way of finding out: to go and see.

Indeed and truly this body is formed of the dust of the earth. Dust it is, and unto dust it doth return when the spirit departs from it. The second great act of creation then was when God made man in His own image, after His own likeness, as we are told in the first account of creation (Gen. 1:26), or as we are told in the second account (Gen. 2:7). These two accounts interweave. God, after He made man out of the dust of the earth (this being the physical body), breathed into man the breath of life so that man became a living soul. The forming of the body of mankind out of the same elements that are in the dust of the earth may have taken untold ages, and out of what forms that body may have grown we do not know. Or indeed, if some can imagine that God made the body of man in an instant, they have a right so to think.

But the spirit of man (that within him that knows himself and that knows God) does not evolve from the dust of the earth, but is breathed into him by the Creator in a separate act of creation. It comes not from the earth by natural ancestry but from heaven by supernatural ancestry. It does not retain within itself the ancient shreds of earth and sea memory that the submerged intelligence of the body retains, but it retains within itself evanescent bits of memory of the heavens from whence it came.

Years ago I memorized a poem which gives one a feeling and an awareness that the conscious mind grasps not at all. I wish I knew the name of the author, to whom I would give great praise. This is the poem:

The Sea

A man has so much water in his hide
He ought to surge with each incoming tide.
And all his cells, like creatures of the deep,
Should glow with phosphorescence in his sleep.
And he should bellow like leviathan.
Though cast ashore on some wave's creamy span
And left to welter age and age ago,
    Great tidal forces in him still can flow:
Sea-water in his veins, and tears of salt.
His ears like conches roar within a vault,
His heart revisits chasms drowned and dim.
The old sea-mother still remembers him.

Something in the deeply submerged unconscious—or perhaps something in the cells of the body—remembers.

There is a bit from Wordsworth's ode, *Intimations of Immortality*, memorized fifty years ago and never forgotten:

Oh joy! that in our embers
Is something that doth live,
That nature yet remembers
What was so fugitive!
The thought of our past years in me doth breed
Perpetual benediction: not indeed
For that which is most worthy to be blest—
Delight and liberty, the simple creed
Of Childhood, whether busy or at rest,
With new-fledged hope still fluttering in his breast:—
    Not for these I raise
    The song of thanks and praise;
    But for those obstinate questionings
    Of sense and outward things,
    Falling from us, vanishings;
    Blank misgivings of a Creature
Moving about in worlds not realized,
High instincts before which our mortal Nature

Did tremble like a guilty thing surprised:
    But for those first affections,
    Those shadowy recollections,
    Which, be they what they may,
Are yet the foundation light of all our day,
Are yet a master light of all our seeing; . . .

Something in the superconscious or the spirit—the breath of life that God breathed into man—remembers.

We are composite beings. We are spirit and we are also flesh. (Gen. 6:3) We are flesh and we are also spirit. And the spirit of man is divided or shared with the spirit of woman, the two being complementary each to each, as we are told symbolically in Genesis 2:21-22.

This is our problem, and it is also our glory. It is the source of all our triumphs and of the miracles of creativity that we have brought forth upon this earth. It is also the source of all our confusion. For we are living in two worlds at once. The world of the spirit, whence come all the archetypes of our creativity, cannot be seen with the eyes of the flesh. Nevertheless, this spiritual reality so invades our being that unless we learn to behold and encompass it with the inward vision of our spirits, we fall into confusion and dismay, being indeed lost souls upon a world whose inner realities we cannot grasp.

The collection of books that we call the Bible is the drama of God and man and of the earth whereupon God established man and to whom He gave dominion over it. (E.g., Matt. 21:33-41) The bits and glimpses that I will pick out in this book and endeavor to illumine with common sense will be those bits that show the interweaving of the three: God and Man and Earth.

2
Adam and Eve

*

We have looked back through time to timelessness, and have considered in a few brief pages the great mystery of the evolving of life from the Word of God. We have considered particularly one rather small heavenly body among billions of heavenly bodies: the planet earth. We have seen the beginning of sentient life in the sea, in the air, upon the land. We have turned our minds to the apex of this sentient life: man.

Here the life of the Spirit of God has probed more deeply than the sciences of creation have yet been able to probe, for we have gone beyond the visible into the invisible world. This supranatural or spiritual world is as real as the more condensed world that we see with our eyes. The more advanced among our scientists are beginning to understand this. It is the world of ideas, of thought-forms, of archetypes, and of spiritual energies. The very essence of the spirit is called in Genesis the "breath of life," and since God Himself breathed into Adam this breath of life, surely it can be called the breath of God. This breath of God cannot be an emanation from a physical body as our breath is, for God is a spirit and does not live in a physical body. This breath of God is therefore of necessity an emanation from God's being or Holy Spirit.

But we do not generally see in man the light and the beneficence that we attribute to God's Holy Spirit. Among the kind and good qualities of man we see an almost unbelievable tendency toward cruelty and evil. Evil is apparently inborn, capable of coming forth without any visible outer influence. A terrifying picture of this "original sin" is given in a modern novel, *Lord of the Flies* by William Golding.

Most perplexingly, this is not an evil that pervades the whole personality, for along with it there is also in man a great capacity for good, and a natural kindness. One cannot say simply that the Koreans, for example, are evil or cruel. This I know from Old China, where I was born and bred. The same people who could take delight in watching death by a hundred tortures could be the kindest and most admirable of men. One finds in these ancient cultures virtues of industry and of courage, of kindness and of an exquisite courtesy far surpassing that of our western culture. The culture of Old China was refined and polished by centuries of training in good manners and morals inculcated by wise teachers such as Confucius. (One does not know how much of this remains; my guess would be that at least the capacity for it is still there, buried beneath an armor of callousness.) But all the wise and virtuous thinking of the sages could not redeem the underlying horror of brutality, as the novels of Lin Yutang and as the study of Chinese history plainly show. Apparently the wisdom of man cannot reach into that part of him that is "flesh."

But why is this submerged evil in the depths of man? It does not have to be so merely because his body was earth-born, evolving through the spaciousness of time upon this planet. The lion is not evil. He does not kill except for food, he does not hurt his own kind, he is not unfaithful to his wives. The dog is not evil. He returns love for love and faithfulness for faithfulness. He forgives injury and turns dislike into love by the ardor of his own love. There is nothing evil about simply being an earth-creature, child of this beautiful planet on which we live! An earth-creature who is also animated by the very breath of God should indeed be a son of God, filled with love and light! Then, *why?* Surely some other influence than the influence of God must have found a way into us!

This is the ancient problem of evil, and I do not claim to have the answer to it. No searchlight is strong enough to penetrate all darkness. The first searchlight I ever saw was in Chefoo harbor in an old forgotten war between Russia and Japan. I would watch, fascinated and a bit frightened, as a beam swept across the sky and picked out here and there pale pools of light. But the rest of the land and the sea remained in darkness.

Our astronauts have this very morning (Dec. 27, 1968, man's first trip around the moon) returned to earth, and they call this small planet an oasis in great blackness. Yet the sea of darkness that they have so wondrously traversed is as nothing beside the horrifying great blackness of interstellar space. Is there anywhere in this illimitable universe a place whence might have come to Adam and Eve another influence than that of God, thus starting the long train of inherited evil in mankind? The same laws of creativity that caused worlds to revolve around our sun must have produced like worlds around thousands of other suns. Can there be living entities upon any of these other planets? If so, are they human or do they appear in quite other forms? Or can it be that such entities live in no form visible to us—that they are, in other words, invisible?

So let us turn the light of commonsense upon some of the bits of illumination given in the Bible concerning an enemy who might have come from outside and sown seeds of evil in the field of God's earth. (Matt. 13:24-30)

We are told that man was tempted by a creature called a serpent. (Gen. 3:1) This creature was not apparently a snake, as we know snakes, for only afterward did he so degenerate as to crawl upon his belly, his mouth in the dust. (Gen. 3:14) What the appearance of this living creature was we do not know. He was more wise than any beast of the field, and he may have been more beautiful. Did he appear in a form similar to man's, or in some other form? Was he a little man with a pointed head? Was he long and sinuous and shadowy like some weird giant? Was he a crawling thing like a lizard, or a crab with purple scales?

Some of you may be thinking, "Why, that sounds like science fiction!" Yes. What we call science fiction is a symptom of man's wonderings about time and space. Unbelievable as such accounts are, and as they are meant to be, they yet show a reaching out to know the reality of life on other planets, about other suns in this incredibly vast universe.

The tempter of Genesis 3 is said to have fallen from heaven. (Isa. 14:12). Jesus described heaven as His Father's home, and He also stated that in His Father's home were many mansions. (John 14:2) Is there any particular reasons why these "many mansions" of heaven must necessarily be floating upon thin air, or is it possible that they are simply other planets around other suns? And if so, is it too utterly ridiculous to wonder whether a creature from one planet might descend upon another planet, even as our astronauts contemplate descending upon the moon?

Yes, I know that this reads like science fiction. And I am inclined to believe that Genesis is one of the most exciting science fiction stories ever written, containing within it truths too deep to be told in literal, straightforward words. I do not reject then the thought that the "serpent" may have been a living creature "planted" or "seeded" on this earth from another earth.

In any case, the tempter, variously called Satan, Lucifer, the Prince of This World, the Dragon, the Father of Lies and other uncomplimentary epithets, is reported as coming from somewhere that we would call outer space. We have already noted the possibility of there being living creatures on other planets around other suns somewhere in this vast universe. But the tempter was an evil being, whether he was a thought-form who appeared in the body of a sinuous creature, or whether he was an actually visible humanoid creature from beyond similar to those described in the book of Revelation. (Rev. 12:3; 13:2, etc.) But if all creation is the work of God, the Creator, and if God is as we assume good, then why should He have created an evil being?

Possibly He did not create an evil being. God created us, according to the Bible, and He made us intrinsically good—after His image. But we may if we like choose to do evil. We are given the power of choosing: free will. Possibly God did not create an evil being but only a nonhuman being with the same power of free choice that we have. The whole story of the Bible would seem to say that this is so. God is the protagonist of this unfinished three-act drama, the Bible. Satan is the villain: the enemy who was originally an archangel and who rebelled against God and so fell from heaven and somehow landed upon this earth. (Isa. 14:12; Rev. 12:7-9)

Of what possible interest was little embryo earth to a fallen prince of God? In order to try to understand this we must look deeper into story of creation and try to see what was the purpose of God the Creator in trying to unite a spiritual being with a physical being and to create a new species upon this earth.

One key to unraveling this mystery is to understand a little bit concerning the nature and being of God, who is the most passionate and persistent of creators. He is delighted and fascinated with the act of creation, both of things inconceivably great and of things unbelievably small. If there were no one there to see the lightning-bugs, He would still create them, for apparently He Himself contemplates them and finds them good. (Gen. 1:4,10,12,18,21,25,31)

Astronomers tell us that there are no lightning-bugs or any other living creatures upon the other planets surrounding our own sun because there is no available air for them to breathe. What God has in mind for Venus and Mars, for instance, we do not know. Nor can we possibly guess what experiments, both great and small, God may be carrying out on other worlds revolving around other suns in galaxies billions of light-years away. But the Creator's crowning experiment upon this planet seems to be to bring forth a being both physical and also spiritual, in hopes that among this race there may evolve the sons of God. (John 1:12) And the story of Genesis seems to indicate that this new species was to be so transformed by its spiritual essence that it could not be subject to death. (Gen. 2:17) Most of us cannot face this glaring impossibility and prefer to take the subject symbolically: to limit immortality to the spirit of man and to exclude the body. Let the body die, we think, but let the spirit become immortal.

This may be the end of the matter; I do not know. That a being visible or capable of becoming visible in a solid body of flesh can pass into the immortal state without going through death seems too fantastic to be true. Yet the wistful dreams of mankind in all ages and in the myths of all peoples hinted at some such possibility as this. So let us train our searchlight upon the very farthest vista of possible truth and see what we can see.

Apparently God had in mind a plan for man's evolving step by step into a being not subject to death. In order that the spiritual body retain the tremendous vigor needed for this transfer, it was necessary for that spirit to remain in direct contact with God, just as it is necessary for the shining of a lamp that it remain in direct contact with the power house whence flows the electricity. Man was not at that time sufficiently developed to understand the whole moral law, nor was there any necessity of his understanding it. But God gave him one command translated in this old story thus: he was not to eat of the tree of the knowledge of good and evil. (Gen. 2:17) This may have been a literal tree having a literal fruit. Or this may be a pictorial way of saying that man was not to absorb into himself and make part of himself (to eat) the knowledge of not only good, but also evil.

That which we eat with the mouth becomes a part of the body, and out of this nourishment the body is made. That which we eat (absorb) with the mind becomes a part of the soul, and out of it the soul or psyche is made. This total absorption with good was a tremendous injunction. Man was not able to obey it. The result of absorbing (eating) the knowledge of evil, even though it was mixed with the knowledge of good, was inevitably to sink lower into the physical body, and thus to put oneself under that law of death which is part of the life-cycle of the physical. So God said to man that in the day (epoch, or period of time) wherein man absorbed this knowledge of evil, man would surely die. And so he does.

The Bible is full of hints of another day—the Day of the Lord—wherein death will be no more. We sing of this loudly in all of our Christian music, from the solemn chant, "If Christ be risen from the dead, then are we also risen with Him," to the plaintive phrase in that most beautiful of all American music, the Negro spiritual, "I ain't a-goin' to die no more."

Those of us who compliment ourselves upon being rationalists have translated this to mean that the two bodies will separate: the physical will die and decay, and the spiritual will live on in a somewhat indeterminate fashion. Maybe so. But Adam and Eve did not consider this to be any big deal, and neither do most of us, if we will tell ourselves the truth!

Genesis glimpses the possibility, mentioned above, of the life of the spiritual so transforming the physical that the two become one—not one physical body, the physical dragging the spiritual down to death, but one resurrection body, the spiritual lifting the physical up to life.

How this could have been done, and what exactly would have happened to the human race if the Tempter had never come and if Adam could have walked only in the knowledge of good, we do not know. Enoch, we are told, "walked with God: and he was not; for God took him." (Gen. 5:24) Elijah went from one manifestation of life to another in an appearance of light like a chariot of fire. (2 Kings 2:11) He was taken away quite literally in an "unidentified flying object"! So far as we can tell from the Bible neither Enoch nor

Elijah left his physical body on earth. There are stories in our present-day life of people who have simply disappeared. We have always believed, however, that some physical calamity befell them beyond the finding out of man. It is not considered intelligent to contemplate the possibility of anything supernatural, anything that cannot be understood with the mind of man.

Well, let us return to Genesis. The results of eating or not eating the knowledge of good and evil are so far beyond us that we take refuge, as I have just done, in humor and fantasy. But the near results of Adam and Eve's disobedience, suggested to them by the Tempter, are immediate and plain to be seen. They become conscious of their lower selves and therefore they promptly hid from God. (Gen. 3:7-8) It is supposed to be a great thing nowadays to know ourselves, and so it is if we know not only our human selves but also our real or spiritual selves: the potentialities within us as sons of God. But if we know only our human selves, understanding more and more what makes us do this and say that, our awareness of God's light in our spirits becomes dimmed and we also, like Adam and Eve, hide more and more from God.

As Adam and Eve became separated from their Creator, they lost the light of God that until this time had shone about them like a garment. Hitherto they had not been aware of their bodies: they had been clothed in light! The original creativity of God that brought forth the worlds in the beginning still shone within them and around about them as it has done around certain saints all through history. (George Fox, in William James's *Varieties of Religious Experience.*) It was through this light—this creative energy—that man was to continue the work of creation. (Gen. 1:28ff.; 2:15) For the light of God, shining through him, would enrich the earth. I do not believe that Adam took care of the Garden of Eden by means of putting bone meal around the tree of life, nor yet by spraying it with DDT. The essence of God through him was life unto the earth, and the balance of nature was preserved so long as the balance of the spirit was preserved in man. But when man fell out of balance, and his light went away from him, and he was naked before God, then something happened to nature itself: the ground no more spontaneously brought forth food for man, but it brought forth thorns and thistles, and man had to till it by the sweat of his brow. The processes of nature no more took place with ease and joy! Eve gave birth to children with pain and travail. (Gen. 3:16) Thus man was driven out of that state of complete beauty and utter goodness that the Bible calls the Garden of Eden into a state of toil and struggle wherein he has been unto this day. The very powers of heaven, called cherubim in this glowing old account of God and man, refused man entry into life and beauty, ease and joy, while his soul was separated from God. (Gen. 3:24)

A parable may be a made-up story carrying a spiritual truth, or it may be a true story carrying a spiritual truth. In the parables of Jesus for instance, maybe there really was a woman who lost a coin (Luke 15:8), and swept the whole house until she found it. Jesus may have used this real story to illustrate the joy of finding one's own soul. There may really have been a father who divided unto his sons his inheritance, and later welcomed the prodigal who had squandered it (Luke 15:11ff.), and Jesus may have used this real incident to illustrate the love of God.

Similarly, there may really have been a Garden of Eden, as tradition said there was, in Mesopotamia between the Tigris and the Euphrates rivers. Through the falling away of man from the balance of God, this garden may truly have lost its fertility, and man may thus have been forced to abandon it. It is not for me to decide these questions. But I have studied forty years in the wilderness of man's problems and of his need for the spiritual laws of God. Therefore, whether or not the incidents of the story are true or symbolic, I know that the laws of God and man and of the planet earth illustrated in this remarkable story are true.

3
Cain and Abel

I know that the workings of God and man and the earth shown in Genesis 1 and 2 are true because I see them in life. The sin of Adam and of Eve was in failing to obey the voice of God, and in listening to another voice. I have done that myself. Once I was driving down the street I passed a house where lived a young woman who had just returned from the hospital after childbirth. She was known to me only in the Players' Club and that very slightly. But a voice within me said, "Go and pray for her." I did not know whether this was God's voice or only a notion of my own, and I talked myself out of it and listened to the voice of my mind. "Don't be silly," said Satan, or my rational mind within me. "She would think you a complete idiot and so you wouldn't be able to help her anyway. Besides, she's just had a baby, that's all. There's no need of rushing in to pray for her."

So I went my way and did not obey the voice of God. And I regret it to this day. For the young woman was on the edge of mental breakdown and if I had gone at that very time she could have been saved. I know. For I went to the mental institution later to see her and she heard me gladly. But I had missed the opportunity which could have resulted in a complete and immediate cure.

In those days I did not know that one could listen to God. But the primitive people Cain and Abel did know. They had no other guide to life than the voice of God. As we hear in the story of the "fall," God spoke to Adam and Eve to give them a warning, as

He so often does today. A friend of mine was driving in the country, and he heard a voice as from the next seat say, "Move over." It was so real that he said, "O.K.," and moved to the side of the road. The next instant a car came over a hill at top speed and in his lane. If he had not obeyed that voice he would have had a head-on crash.

Another friend was going with his wife on a drive to Texas. He had a strong disinclination to take the trip. His mind became heavier and heavier as the time drew near. But he did not know that this was a warning from God's Spirit within him, nor did the friend to whom he told his feeling realize that this was the case. "Oh, as soon as you get started, you'll have a wonderful time," said she.

But he did not. A car came over a hill in his lane and he and his wife were killed.

How often we say afterward, "If I had only followed my hunch!"

What is a hunch but the voice of God's Spirit in our own unconscious mind warning or guiding us? We have not learned the simple act of listening. But we can learn. We can go apart, sit quietly, fold our hands, close our eyes, put all else from our minds and simply listen. And if there comes to us a word of warning, we would be wise to obey it.

To illustrate this, I wish to quote a verse from William Cullen Bryant's poem "To a Waterfowl," memorized long ago.

He who from zone to zone
    Guides through the boundless sky thy certain flight
In the long way that I must tread alone
    Will lead my steps aright.

Well, I am not so sure, because the waterfowl presumably heeds that voice within him which we call instinct and veers not from the path that it directs, whereas we would be very likely to question that voice. "Why should I always go the same way?" we might ask. "I think it would be more fun to try a different route this time. I might locate a reedy brook that no other bird knows about, and then what a lot of fish I'd catch! And I won't tell them about it either." And we just might, assuming falsely that all bodies of land were replete with waterbrooks, come to earth exhausted in the middle of the Sahara Desert—a poor place for waterfowl.

Thus are we different from all other created animals. We also have that voice within us that we might call instinct or a "hunch." But it is not a blind hunch. For we have minds wherewith to think and wills wherewith to choose.

As we have seen, there came to Adam and to Eve a word of warning. They should not eat of the tree of the knowledge of good and evil. It might quite simply have been a real tree whose fruit would harm them, as the fruit of the olive tree, until processed, poisons one who eats it. Or Eve's tempting Adam to eat the "apple" (nowhere in the Bible is it called an apple, by the way) might have been symbolic of some other deviation from God's laws. But the woman and then the man chose to listen not to God's warning but to the Tempter.

This was the beginning of their losing contact with God, as we have previously noted. They could not pass on to their children that which they did not have, any more than we can. Therefore as years and centuries passed, their children became less and less aware of the voice of God within them.

Nevertheless, their children or descendants still had a yearning for God and needed the sense of His acceptance or approval. From time to time a voice within would intimate to them by a feeling of discomfort that their actions were not acceptable to their Creator. Then they would fall back upon the idea of propitiating the deity with some kind of an offering. The formal sacrifice of an animal was accepted by the priests of the Jewish temple centuries after this ancient story, but we have no way of knowing how early in history the idea of a burnt offering occurred to man. Heathen religions carried this way of propitiating the gods even to the horrifying extent of human sacrifices. And we find it symbolized in the Christian religion by the sacrifice of the mass or the communion service, typifying Christ's offering of Himself upon the cross.

Cain, then, offered upon an altar the fruits of his field and Abel offered a lamb from his flock. And we are told that God accepted Abel's offering but did not accept Cain's. (Gen. 4:4-5) This seems very notional of God. So let us consider what the inner meaning of these words may be. Cain, feeling a sense of guilt or dissatisfaction within himself, thought to win God's favor by offering some of his crops upon an altar and burning them up with fire. The concept of an object ascending to heaven when burned is a very ancient one. I have seen in China paper money and even paper menservants and maidservants being carried in a funeral procession to be burned at the graves, so that the essence of them could ascend in smoke into the heavens and be there transformed into supply and service. But Cain looked upon his younger brother Abel, who was offering a lamb, and promptly felt a dissatisfaction with his own offering and a jealousy of his brother's. Whether this feeling came from God I do not know. But possibly he did not translate God's message quite correctly. God may have been saying, "Yes, I see your sacrifice, but you have in your heart hate and jealousy toward your brother and of that you have not repented. Therefore your sacrifice is but a vain form."

I do not think that I am being too fanciful to write this, for obviously Cain did have this hate in his heart. For at this point he picked up a rock and killed his brother. (Gen. 4:8) Such hate does not spring fullborn into a person's mind, but grows with the years. It could be that from childhood Cain had felt that his parents loved Abel more than they loved him, or that Abel was more gifted and more righteous than he was, and so instead of loving and revering his brother for superior qualities he had been jealous of him—having the false assumption that so many people have today, namely, that all people are equal or should be. (This is manifestly absurd. Can all people sing like Marian Anderson, or play baseball like Joe DiMaggio, or fly to the moon?)

Thus Cain in his dissatisfaction with himself hated his brother who was more spiritual than he was, and killed him. Nor did he repent of his action. "Where is Abel thy brother?" (Gen. 4:9) said the voice of God within him, sounding this time loud and clear, because whether Cain wanted to do so or not, he was uneasily listening for that voice. (This I know, because all of us do so.)

And Cain said, "I know not: Am I my brother's keeper?" (Gen. 4:9)

It did him no good, this denial, because there was a witness to this murder: the earth itself into which the blood of Abel soaked. "The voice of thy brother's blood crieth unto me from the ground" (Gen. 4:10), said the Lord, and there was no mistaking His voice this time, for the thunder of it filled the heavens. "And now art thou cursed from the earth," said Jehovah, Creator and Judge. "When thou tillest the ground, it shall not henceforth yield unto thee her strength; a fugitive and a vagabond shalt thou be in the earth." (Gen. 4:11-12) And so he was. He could not make a living anywhere because the earth itself refused to cooperate with him. The hatred in his heart reflected itself upon the earth, which sought means of revenging itself upon him.

So the earth itself rejected Cain. Nevertheless, man was not allowed to kill him, for that would only have increased upon the earth the curse of blood shed in violence. God therefore put a mark upon him so that all men should see and know that although sinning, he still belonged to God. (Gen. 4:15)

How on earth could God put a mark upon him with such meaning that no one dared to touch him?

There was a missionary in China long ago who talked with a wise and gentle Buddhist monk.

"Is it really possible," asked the missionary, "that

your magicians and soothsayers can pronounce a curse
upon a person so that he dies?"

"Oh yes," smiled the monk, fanning himself gently
with a palm-leaf fan.

"Has this ever been done to one of us missionaries?"

"Impossible, impossible," replied the monk.

"Why is it impossible?"

"Do you not know? All of you have on your fore-
head a shining *ten*. Therefore we know that we cannot
do this to you."

The missionary was puzzled until he remembered
that the Chinese character for the number ten is almost
a cross. So although they themselves were not sensitive
enough to see it, God had put a mark upon their fore-
heads.

But were there really a Cain and an Abel and later
on, a very superior son, Seth, given to Adam and Eve
in their old age to console them for the loss of Abel?
I see no reason why not. One may, if one chooses, refuse to believe any of this, but I do not so choose. Nor
do I concern myself unduly with whom Seth married
that he should have descendants. (Gen. 5:3-4) Adam
lived we are told nine hundred and thirty years and
begat sons and daughters—scads of them! Nowadays
geneticists have found it unwise for siblings to wed,
because if there is an inherited weakness in the family
the chances of its being passed on are thus doubled.
But in those early days there were no inherited weak-
nesses. Many generations pass before there is a single
record of death from any other cause than the wearing
out of the body in extreme old age. (Gen. 11:28) It
was customary for Egyptian and Hawaiian royalty to
marry brothers and sisters, and there seems to be no
reason why the men of old should not also have done
so. Indeed, Abraham's wife was his half-sister, nor
did anyone think ill of that. (Gen. 20:12)

However, though I consider this story of Cain and
Abel true, I do see in it a prototype of human behavior
from that day to this. When we feel ourselves inferior
or are in some way dissatisfied with ourselves, instead

of recognizing our faults and our lacks and coping with them, we project our dissatisfaction with ourselves upon someone else. We think it is the other person and not ourselves who is mean or hateful or cruel. So instead of rooting out that evil in ourselves, we try to destroy it in somebody else—and as often as not, destroy not only the evil but also the person, as Cain did.

But we cannot kill evil by killing a person or people. For the evil clings to the very earth whereon we live and there it will breed more evil. History shows us this fact in glaring and tragic pictures and yet we do not heed its warning, but continue to kill our brothers of other tribes and nations. And the voice of our brother's blood cries ever louder to its Creator from the ground.

"The evil that men do lives after them," said the prophet Shakespeare.

How can this be?

Words do not die. The cry of rage from the murderer, and of anguish from the murdered, fade out from the ear, but not from the heart. The finer vibrations of them remain in the air and, though not audible to the ear, are sensible to the heart. They can be felt though they cannot be heard. Even thoughts can be felt though they cannot be heard. And the more emotion there is behind the thoughts, the more they permeate and influence the air and the earth. Therefore the Bard of Avon said that while men's evil in the violence of its emotion is apt to live after them, "The good is oft interred with their bones."

But not always—not always. And it is possible to make constructive thoughts so powerful that they will out-cry the influences of evil.

Now in case you are thinking, "How can she know this?" I say to you, "Listen."

For you also can feel in the air and in the earth the presence of evil, or of good. Be aware of your feelings. Listen to your own heart. All of us have heard of haunted houses, houses full of a sense of uneasiness and apparently of an influence of evil. My brother once lived in such a house. "What is it?" he said to me.

"Everything has gone wrong since we moved to this house!"

This I did not doubt, for depression had settled upon me like a cloud as soon as I set foot through its front door.

"Find out who lived here before you and what happened in this house," I suggested.

It transpired that a most unhappy family had lived there and that a suicide had taken place in the very room where we sat. The house was indeed haunted, not necessarily by a personality but certainly by the accumulated thought-vibrations of evil that had soaked into the very walls.

"But we can't move out!" said my brother. "We've taken a lease!"

Therefore we went from room to room and in every room we made the sign of the cross, as though to break the thought-currents of evil. And we commanded in the name of Jesus Christ that all evil, personal or impersonal, should leave that house and that it should be filled with the love of Christ. And the house became habitable from that time forth.

Can thought-vibrations actually permeate a building? Apparently they can. I used to attend the Philadelphia Orchestra concerts every Friday afternoon and, being unable to afford a season ticket, would usually sit upon the stone steps and lean against the red brick wall and wait for a fifty-cent ticket to the concert hall. One afternoon while waiting there my feelings changed. I became swept into that state of unalloyed bliss that was mine when the glorious orchestra under the baton of Stokowski filled the auditorium with the pulsing rhythm of music. And I realized that the very walls of the building were soaked with those vibrations.

On the other hand there are houses that I cannot abide in, for the hate and ugliness that have filled their walls surge upon me in a feeling of black depression.

Moreover, not only buildings can be thus saturated, whether with good or with evil, but even the earth itself can cry out to us, either with the anguish of the

blood of our brothers slain upon it or with the peace of
God somehow abiding there. We would do well to
understand this. I have known Americans of a certain
sensitivity who have blithely gone to Germany to study
and who have returned utterly shattered, a prey to
fear and depression for which they find no cause. But
there is a cause. The blood of six million Jews is crying
to God from that country's ground, and their spirits
hear it although their ears do not. On the other hand,
there remain places upon the earth, and I have found
them particularly in our own most fortunate country,
where the original peace of God still lives and moves,
and where one's heart finds comfort merely by walking
upon the good earth, and resting upon its cool grass
and beneath its whispering trees. Such a place upon a
dirt road unopened to buildings struck my fancy in the
little town of Westboro. "I'd like to build a house right
here," I said to my husband. We did not do so. But
some years later when looking for a home we found a
house upon this exact spot, and immediately both of
us knew it for a place of peace and bought it for our
home. A young woman of the town once looked
through my kitchen window and cried out, "Oh, there
it is! The path up the hill! When I felt depressed I always came here and walked up that little path and I
found peace!"

And in case this sounds too utterly fanciful, let me
again refer you to the works of that great pre-historian
and anthropologist, Pierre Teilhard de Chardin, who
states that the very spirit and presence of God are in
all created things.

The earth then can be filled with the presence of God
and lit with His light and with His peace. But another
influence has entered into it, so that apparently it tries
to breed destruction for the men upon it. In the beginning illness was not known. Plants and animals lived
their life-cycle and died, but man lived on for hundreds
of years, due I suppose to the light of God still within
him, and died only when the body was quite worn out
with age. Bacteria existed upon the earth but performed

only the useful duties of transforming decayed objects upon the earth into sources of new life and of helping man to digest his food. On the contrary, nowadays germs and bacteria seem to increase and multiply and transform themselves into more and more virulent causes of death and destruction. And this takes place in spite of all the wonderful discoveries of modern medicine.

What is this protest against mankind that comes apparently from the very earth whereon we live? Is it still the voice of our brothers' blood crying to us from the ground? How then shall it be answered, and what will still its crying?

That is rather a large question for us to consider so soon. As the story of God and man and the earth unfolds in the Bible we may be better able to attempt an answer. We will from time to time train our searchlight upon this question, which really concerns the healing of the planet earth: the redeeming of sin and sickness. Many of us have wondered why this person or that person was not healed in spite of prayer and faith. There is much righteous rejoicing about those who are healed in evangelistic services, for instance, and rightly so. But what of those who are not healed—those who come weary miles in wheelchairs and return weary miles in the same wheelchairs? Is it just or kind to dismiss the matter by saying, "They did not have enough faith?" Or is it possible that the earth itself was attacking them with its viruses and its malignancies, and that the attack was so sore that only by the healing of the disease-principle upon the earth could they be healed?

I do not know, but I know that we are called upon to pray for the healing of this earth: "Thy kingdom come, thy will be done on earth as it is in heaven." (Matt. 6:10)

The first step in healing is diagnosis. We have briefly considered what the evil and the violence of man toward man has done to the earth. Now let us also consider, before we turn our minds back to the Word of God, the harm that we have done to the country we live in by our selfish and misguided treatment of it.

We have so polluted lakes by industrial wastes that they no longer cleanse themselves, nor can they be cleansed in any way that man has yet discovered. Some of our rivers are so filled with decay that no life can abide in them, and their shores are lined with dead fish from which arises into the air a sickening miasma, so that people who live nearby become ill with "viruses." The air of our cities is often so polluted that people feel it in their lungs and in their noses and in their eyes, and the end is not yet. The grass of our fields is dimly poisoned with the fall of radiation whose cumulative dangers to the genes of man no one at present knows. We spray our crops with poison that man is supposed to be able to tolerate. But who can know how much he can tolerate, and for how long? And who knows how many of the degenerative diseases of man stem from the sickness of the earth upon which he lives?

The serpent told Eve that if she ate of the tree of the knowledge of good and evil, she would become like God, knowing good from evil. The ironic thing is that man was destined to become like God in his knowing, and if he had waited God's time, this would have come to pass through the slow rolling of the ages in ways that we do not know. We are wont to think consolingly that if man had never sinned, he would have remained an embryo soul, never knowing good from evil. But this is not in accord with that principle of evolving, of growing from one stage to another stage, that God has built into His world. Man was tempted to do wrong that good might come, to bring about a reform or a growth of his soul by breaking God's commandments, just as man is still tempted to do wrong that good may come.

The old temptation still remains! The old sin is still committed: to create a world of peace by bombing those who oppose us, to bring about social reforms by planting seeds of hate and violence, to steal and lie and cheat in order to build up great fortunes and endow hospitals.

Whatever the hidden pictures behind this old history of God and man, the truth of it remains and is obvious: man yielded to the temptation to break God's laws and to exalt his own wisdom, and to do things his own way, not waiting for God. And we to this day inherit this tendency, and therefore are under condemnation.

Did God in His wisdom know that man would thus step out on his own, and would need that work of redemption possibly foreshadowed in Genesis 3:15? I cannot answer this question, the old problem of man's free will and God's foreknowledge. All I know is that the Creator was not willing to lose His gamble in making man in His own image after His own likeness. (Gen. 1:26) And if the original way of putting him in a garden and providing for him a tree of life did not work, then He had in mind another way, the way of the cross.

We read in this old story that the invisible energy of the earth was changed by the violence of man. And from the earth and by the earth Cain was punished. The earth no longer brought forth its increase for his use. (Gen. 4:12) He wandered from here to there, and nature itself in its refusal to cooperate with him kept him wandering.

But could not he have healed the wounds that he had made upon the earth? No, he could not. I once read the "lost books" of the Bible—rather boring as a whole, and by no means equal to those ancient manuscripts that men of old chose to put together into the history of God and man that we call the Bible. But there was one book, the story of Adam and Eve, that contained some food for thought. Adam and Eve mourned continually for the garden, and for the "bright nature" that they had lost; but not all their tears and cries could restore to them their heritage. Jesus Christ had not yet come to the earth to mingle His blood with the blood of Abel who was slain, and to redeem the earth. Therefore Cain's brother's blood continued to cry to the Creator from the ground.

But now the Redeemer has come.

4
Noah

✗

Genesis, Chapter 6, shows us what the end may be. The earth became so polluted by the evil imagination of men's hearts that it shrugged its shoulders and cast off its living creatures. God's Spirit had striven long with man, seeing man as a being in His image, after His likeness. "There were giants in the earth in those days . . . mighty men . . . men of renown." (Gen. 6:4) Some think that there was a civilization advanced in wisdom and might, more advanced than we are today, and that it destroyed itself, or was destroyed by the inexorable laws of God—and the two mean the same thing. There was a tremendous cataclysm of nature; the "fountains of the great deep [were] broken up." (Gen. 7:11) This was followed by such a disturbance, of the winds and the jet stream and the distribution of waters upon the earth, that it rained for forty days. It was months after that before the waste of mud dried out enough to support life.

In the days when I began teaching the Bible I used to say that of course neither Noah nor Moses knew the size of the earth, and that probably the flood that, as the Bible says, "covered the earth" actually covered only the region around the Mediterranean Sea. Thus in our ignorance we tend to limit and to narrow this ancient collection of books.

For now I know better. Mankind is beginning to remember. There are ever-increasing legends of the destruction of an ancient civilization, and of the lost continent upon which it developed, the continent of Atlantis, from which the Atlantic Ocean is named. There are even dim, drifting tales of another lost civilization, the continent of Lemuria. I do not say that I swallow these old tales "hook, line and sinker," nor that I know whether these hypothetical wise men of old blew up their world with atomic energy or destroyed it by misdirected psychic powers. I do not know whether Stonehenge dates from some remnant of a forgotten civilization, or whether the island of Iona is a bit of that lost continent, or whether the Aztec Indians derived their ancient wisdom from some once-submerged life remaining in a fragmented way upon the earth.

But I do accept what the old story of Genesis, Chapter 6, tells me: the imagination of men's hearts, the evil thought-forms engendered by a fallen mankind, were displeasing to the Creator. Therefore He permitted the earth to destroy mankind, possibly by shifting on its axis either due to an internal explosion, or due to the continual giving-off of magnetism, or due simply to disgust with man! Some people believe that this very thing happened: the earth flipped upon its axis, so that the North Pole became a tropic region. If this theory be true, the ice of the poles would melt in tropic heat and the waters would be hurled by the rotation of the earth across the continents in a great tidal wave engulfing all the land and all the hills. And until nature had settled itself again, this would obviously be followed by the continual rising of moisture into the air, and its coming down again in the form of rain.

Most people, of course, would not accept this theory. It is a disconcerting thing to believe, especially as the scientists who support it casually remark that the earth has done this flip more than once, and that any time now it may do it again. I do not say that you must believe it, but I suggest that you put it alongside Genesis, Chapters 6-9, and see what you see.

First of all, the psychic reasons for this calamity were made very plain: the earth was corrupt, and the earth was filled with violence. This was the out-picturing of the inner cause of calamity, which was that "the

imagination of man's heart is evil from his youth."
(Gen. 8:21) "God looked upon the earth, and, behold,
it was corrupt." (Gen. 6:12) The blood of many
brothers cried to God from the ground, and God
heard their cry and cleansed the earth quite literally
with water, so that the evil thought-forms created by
man were washed away from it, and humanity had another chance—a new beginning through one man. Noah.
He was a "just man and perfect in his generations, and
Noah walked with God" (Gen. 6:9), and his children
were brought up in the knowledge of God. God
warned Noah of what would happen to the earth, and
guided him to create a ship of such dimensions that it
could float atop the waters and sustain life until the flood
had subsided.

But why didn't God warn everybody and give them
another chance? Surely if they knew of such danger
to their earth, they might repent, or at least build themselves a boat! It is possible that the warning was there
in the earth, and that any who walked with God, as
Noah did, could catch it. The spirit of man lives beyond time and space, and the spirit of man can perceive things to come, and thus can often protect him
in one way or another. Even the "instinct" of animals
often warns them of danger. I heard of a deep, unsea-
sonable freeze in the south when no birds were frozen
because all had left the area two days before the cold
spell came. Sailors tell of rats who leave a ship that is
headed for disaster. There are countless stories of
people who have sensed a warning voice and have followed it and saved their lives. I know a young man who
planned to fly to a foggy island in the north Pacific.
He inquired of the Lord, and listened, and the Lord
said, "Do not fly on Tuesday." On Tuesday the plane
crashed, and all were killed. Why did God not warn
the other passengers of danger. Quite likely He did.
The imminence of storm was in the air for any to
catch, if their spirits were sufficiently sensitive. In other
words, His warning was there, but they did not ask
Him—they did not listen.

Noah, then, felt the uneasiness of the earth, and as he walked with God he was able to catch the guidance of the Lord, and to act upon it. How do I know that Noah felt the uneasiness of the earth? Because I have felt it myself three or four days before an earthquake or a tornado. I am gradually learning to put my finger on the deep uneasiness, and say to the Lord, "What is it, and what shall I do?" Of course! This kind of foreknowledge is available to all who walk with God.

It is very possible that Noah told other people of his uneasiness, and that they did not believe him. Certainly Isaiah and Jeremiah in their day warned the people of coming destruction, and those people would not heed nor repent. God told Noah, moreover, how to build a seaworthy craft—and surely there is nothing strange in this! We also build seaworthy craft, and if we listen to God, His inspiration can help us in this and every creative venture. God also told Noah to take with him into the ark two of every living creature, in order to preserve life upon the earth. (Gen. 6:19) In the similar account of Genesis 7:2ff. we are told that Noah was to take seven of the domestic beasts usable by man and two of every other kind, even the wild beasts of the field, in order to preserve a balance of nature.

People have had a lot of fun with Noah and his ark, making toys of wood to represent the animals marching up a gangplank into the ark, and even preserving this old story in animal crackers. Until I learned to pin my attention to the Bible, and not to old wives' fables, I puzzled greatly about this, visioning Noah stalking through the forests in search of tigers, or lassoing buffalo in order to lug them up that gangplank. But actually it would not be like this at all. Any creature surviving the first great upheaval would swim or fly toward that ark. The only question would be what to let in, and what to beat off. If Noah had not hearkened unto the Lord, he would probably have helped cattle and sheep to scramble out of the water and into the great doorway upon the side of the ark (Gen. 6:16), and would assiduously have kept out lions. But God knew that for the working out of His great universe lions also were needed.

If he had not walked with God, Noah might have been afraid to let lions come panting and dripping aboard the ark, and shake water all over his sons, Shem, Ham, and Japheth, and over their respective wives. But God knew that in times of emergency there is no violence among the creatures. The deer and the panther herd together on a bit of an island amid the roaring furnace of a forest fire, and do not fight. As for the problem of feeding all these animals, that I shall not attempt to puzzle out, anymore than I would attempt to puzzle out ways of feeding several thousand people aboard Queen Elizabeth II. One hopes that in such a time of shock, the animals appetites were poor! At any rate, the picture of a floating vessel, and creatures swimming or flying to it in hopes of refuge, is far more sensible than the childish picture of Noah lining up the animals two by two upon dry land.

I once, in a spirit of good clean fun, propounded this theory to a fundamentalist brother, and he was extremely shocked. "But *the Bible says,*" he began, and then shut his mouth quickly, realizing to his credit that the Bible does not say that Noah lined up the animals two by two and marched them along the gangplank. Yes, we were brought up on that concept, but we did not get it from Holy Scripture. We probably got it from a children's toy. When we begin to separate the truth of the Bible from childish fables then maybe our understanding will be enlightened.

Very quaintly we are told that before the flood God remembered that man was not only a spiritual being, he was also a human being: "For that he also is flesh," (Gen. 6:3) "And it repented the Lord that He had made man on the earth, and it grieved Him at His heart." (Gen. 6:6) The ancient writer actually suggests that the Creator looked upon His venture of putting together a spiritual being and a physical being, and said to Himself, "That wasn't such a good idea after all. I wish I had never tried it." Who knows, for who can read the mind of God? Nevertheless, God did not give up His venture completely, but cleansed it and began again.

God then gave to man a solemn command: man was never again to pollute the earth with his brother's blood. "And surely your blood of your lives will I require; . . . whoso sheddeth man's blood, by man shall his blood be shed: for in the image of God made he man." (Gen. 9:5-6)

As we know all too well, however, once more the earth is faced with destruction. Again the blood of our brothers cries to us from the ground, and the inexorable law goes on: whoso sheds man's blood, by man shall his blood be shed. Once more man has corrupted his way upon the earth. There are predictions by seers and scientists of great earthquakes, of parts of continents sliding into the sea, of the earth again flipping on its axis.

What then shall we do? Walk with God, like Noah, and listen! He may remind us first of all that He gave to Noah a solemn promise and covenant, symbolized by His rainbow (Gen. 9:13ff.), that never again would He destroy the earth for man's sake, and even though the imagination of his heart be evil from his youth, neither would He ever again smite everything living as He had done. "While the earth remaineth, seedtime and harvest, and cold and heat, summer and winter, and day and night shall not cease." (Gen. 8:22) It comforts us to remember this.

Nevertheless the fact remains that there is a direct connection between the imagination of man's heart and the earthly atmosphere, in which it breeds either good or evil. And the original commandment of God to man still holds: we are to have dominion over this earth; we are to take control; we are to save it "from the bondage of corruption into the glorious liberty of the children of God." (Rom. 8:21)

It is God's will that the earth shall be saved from utter destruction, and become an ideal society, a kingdom of heaven. This shall come to pass through the sons of God, the children of God, Christians, those who are called by His name. (Rom. 8:14ff.) But how are we, as His representatives on earth, to bring about a kingdom of heaven? We are apt to think, first, of all manner of social reforms, even as the people of Jesus' day thought. They wanted Him to lead a revolution and set His people free from the slavery of the Roman Empire. But He would not do it, for He knew that without the other freedom, the freedom of the spirit of man, it would not work. It was necessary, first, for man to think of himself as a son of God, to know his spiritual dominion over the earth, before it would be safe for him to assume mental and physical dominion. Since the evil imagination of man was the first cause of world disaster, surely we can see that the first reform should be the transformation of the imagination of man's heart to a source of good instead of a source of evil.

As a man "thinketh in his heart, so is he." (Prov. 23:7) We have found, laboriously taught in my other books, that if we think of ourselves as weak and sickly, we become weak and sickly. And if we are thus ill, the greatest step we can take toward health is to change the picture in our hearts, and make within us the picture of ourselves well and strong. Thus we open a door through which God's grace, and the help of His physicians, can heal us. I need hardly repeat here that this does not always work. In some cases the damage is too great, or the weight of our sins against the earth is too heavy, and the healing is best accomplished on the other side. But to correct the imagination of heart is one great step toward health, though naturally it must be accompanied by other steps as we are guided—by proper medical care, if such is needed; by some change in diet or in our way of life; and most of all by some change in our attitudes toward others.

Now let us apply this same method of changing the imagination of the heart to the sickness of the world. The world is made up of all of us who live upon it.

Then, if we think of the world as full of evil, and see it going continually from bad to worse and from worse to terrible, so it will go. "But it *is* evil," you are thinking. Yes. And if you are sick, you *are* sick, and there is nothing to be gained by refusing to admit that fact. Having admitted it, however, then we have learned to make in our minds the picture of health, and take what steps we can toward helping the picture to come true.

Yes, the world is sick, but Jesus taught us to pray that it be healed. "Thy kingdom come. Thy will be done in earth, as it is in heaven." (Matt. 6:10) Cain could not take away the stain of his brother's blood from the ground, but in Jesus, God Himself came to earth, and shed His blood willingly to take away the poison of condemnation from the earth. (Rom. 8:1) The power of His sacrifice is now released to the earth, and it is for us to apply it.

Jesus was no wishful thinker, nor did He say to us, "Cheer up; this is the best of all possible worlds." He told us truly of great tribulation to come, so that we would face reality and be prepared to overcome it. But even through all of this He saw the kingdom of heaven being established upon the earth, so that He said, "And when these things begin to come to pass, then look up, and lift up your heads; for your redemption draweth nigh." (Luke 21:28)

So let us lift up our heads, and let us apply to the world that work of the healing creative imagination that we have learned to apply to other problems of life. Let us make in our minds the picture of a world at peace, men beating "Their swords into plowshares, and their spears into pruninghooks." (Isa. 2:4) That would mean, in modern words, men turning their munitions works into factories for the producing of industrial tools, and their atomic plants into plants for the release of a driving energy to replace oil and gas when that replacement shall become necessary, as it will.

That would be a sort of Utopia, you are perhaps thinking. Yes, but a God-made Utopia, not a man-made one: a world fashioned according to God's laws of diversity which run through all creation, sentient and nonsentient. In our picture of the earth healed and saved from destruction, let us "see" men employed in useful activity, each after the pattern of his nature, as Jesus suggests in the parable of the talents (Matt. 25:14ff.) each earning the measure of money that he proved himself capable of managing. Let us see men learning to love and to appreciate each other, and to get along together. And let us rejoice in all the ways in which this is already coming to pass. And I look forward to the time when men shall learn to work together in the same way that they play together, using the talents of each where they are best fitted, working with each other or for each other to make a more exciting world.

As Pierre Teilhard de Chardin so beautifully says, God is interested in the world that we are building, as a father is interested in a child's house of blocks. God, being a creator, has put us into this world in order to create, and as we build factories and bridges and schools, and make the world beautiful with parks, we are delighting His heart, as well as our hearts.

So now let us make in our minds a world where the goodness of labor is recognized, where men lift up their hearts and know that they can earn their daily bread, where men of means look for honest work that they can offer to honest workers, and where the genius that God gave to man can flower into a world at peace.

Of course there is much more to do than just this creative imagining. But until the imagination of our hearts is healed, much of our doing is of no avail. For as long as we fix our minds on the wickedness of people, even our efforts to help or reform them are apt to be undertaken in a spirit of anger and hate, and thus they profit us nothing. (1 Cor. 13:3) Let us hold in our minds, then, the picture of the world as the kingdom of God, and holding this in our minds, let us refrain from speaking words that go forth to destroy. For every thought-form of evil that we send forth from our lips, saying, "The world is worse than ever," tends to create evil, or at least to fasten upon the world the evil that at present clings to it, instead of drawing toward it the good that is God's will. Moreover, let us not listen to such conversation, but absent ourselves from it in every way possible. For if we listen in silence, it is apt to fasten itself upon us, and if we argue about it, we may create anger, to the detriment of our prayers.

Jesus did not listen to subversive talk, nor did He argue about it. He taught the truth where the way was open for Him to teach the truth. And for the rest, He simply went His way, and gave His life for the bringing into the world of the Holy Spirit of God.

Remember therefore the promises: "And it shall come to pass afterward, that I will pour out my spirit upon all flesh; and your sons and your daughters shall prophesy, your old men shall dream dreams, your young men shall see visions." (Joel 2:28) "For the earth shall be full of the knowledge of the Lord as the waters cover the sea." (Isa. 11:9)

5
Abraham

✳

Abraham was a practical mystic. Someone many years ago called me a practical mystic, and I was amazed, for I did not know what the word "mystic" meant. But I suppose I am one, for it means someone who listens to God, not merely for spiritual benefit but in order to get God's work done upon this earth.

God's work upon this world, as we shall see from the story of Abraham, is not by any means limited to preaching or teaching. Abraham was not a preacher. He was a nomadic herdsman. He listened to God, and God told him to arise and go forth out of his father's house, to a land whither he would lead him. I used to think that this was a very great sacrifice, and indeed, maybe it was. But nowadays we would say that God was simply directing him to a place where his flocks and herds would prosper and his descendants would be established. God, as always, was sensible. Abraham was seventy-five years old, and if he was ever to go forth, it was high time.

Abraham had absolutely no way to ascertain the will of God except through the communication that came to him as he listened: a voice heard in his mind, or in a vision, or in a dream, or through the appearance of an angel. He did not have the Scriptures; the Bible was not written. He did not have the Ten Commandments; the laws of Moses had not as yet been given. Therefore we need not be too surprised if Abraham did not always hear the voice of God correctly. When you read the story (Gen. 12ff.) you may be surprised to find that Abraham's domestic and family life left a great deal to be desired. His wife, Sarah, was a beautiful woman, but apparently quite a problem to him. She was so beautiful that she was a danger. Twice we are told that Abraham passed her off as his sister rather than as his wife, naïvely enough, so that if the king should desire her he would not feel that he must needs kill Abraham, but could just simply take her, and everybody would be happy. The second time, indeed, the king reproved Abraham for thus deceiving him, and Abraham said, "And yet indeed she is my sister; she is the daughter of my father, but not the daughter of my mother; and she became my wife." (Gen. 20:12) To us this seems very strange indeed, but in those old days the human strain had not become weakened, and therefore the laws concerning marriage were not so stringent as they have since become.

God promised Abraham that He would establish a kingdom from his descendants. (E.g., Gen. 17:4) But his wife, Sarah, had no children. Was this a purposeful test of Abraham's faith? Or was the long delay in fulfilling this promise due to God's desire that the child, when he was finally born, should inherit the hardwon faith of Abraham? We do not know. Abraham pled with God that the child of his concubine should be accepted as his descendant, but God refused, insisting that only through the union of Abraham and Sarah would the new nation be born. (Gen. 17:17-21)

In all the Bible we find a tremendous value placed upon inheritance. God plants the seed of a spiritual species, and it is nurtured and developed through generations and generations. And the value of inheritance, which we are apt to ignore except indeed in horses and dogs, is still true.

At any rate, it was only when Sarah was ninety years old that she conceived. No wonder she laughed behind the door at the angel's announcement that she would give birth to a child! (Gen. 18:10-15) In spite of her mirth, however, Isaac was born. The laughter of man does not prevent God's promises from being fulfilled.

The best-known story concerning Abraham is that of his offering Isaac as a sacrifice to the Lord. (Gen. 22:1ff.) The Lord told him to take his son, his only son whom he loved, and put him upon an altar and kill him. This story has been perplexing to many people.

If God spoke to Abraham, He can also speak to us. Any of us have a right, moreover, to go to Him with this story and other stories that perplex us and say, "Lord, give me the key; what is it?" and to listen. Moses, who wrote down this story, did not have the picture of God as a loving Father. Jesus had not yet come to tell men of God's love. The God that Moses knew was a fierce and jealous Jehovah.

Some of you who read this book are fathers. Would you test the faith of your son by asking him to kill your grandson as a sacrifice to God, or for any reason whatsoever? Of course you would not. Well, then, how could God have demanded this of Abraham in order to test his faith? Is God less loving and less good than you are?

Forgive me if I ponder upon this matter. You do not need to accept the results of my pondering, but nevertheless I shall write them down because to some of you they may open a new door. It may be—I do not say that it is, but I say it *may* be—that upon this occasion Abraham heard God partially but not fully. I have had this happen in my own life. The very first time that I went forth on an errand of healing I felt absolutely sure that I was guided to go to a certain young man, schizophrenic, manic depressive, and paranoid, to lay hands on him and to pray for his healing. The venture failed, completely and tragically and permanently. For three months I was cast into darkness. I doubted God.

It was a long time before I came to understand that I had heard God, but not quite accurately. God was saying to me, "Do you see this young man, and his great need of the healing of the mind and soul? I want you to learn to help people in trouble such as his." I did not catch the fullness of God's guidance, nor did I grasp its time sequence. But I obeyed as I did hear and therefore, I am sure, God counted my obedience as righteousness and did not blame me for the failure.

The Bible is a true book. It does not make all its great men idols of perfection, but reports their thoughts and deeds with devastating accuracy. These books of the Bible give us also a picture of man's slowly developing understanding of God. If we today want to know the true nature of God, we go of course to His Son Jesus Christ. We rejoice in the obedience of dear old Abraham, but we do not revert to his concept of God, and kill our firstborn sons to please Him.

It may be that Abraham pondered upon the heathen around him and their ritual of human sacrifice. Possibly another voice, not God's, said to Abraham, "Look at these people. They offer their firstborn sons as sacrifices to Baal or Moloch. Do you love God less than they love their gods? If they are willing to make this sacrifice, aren't you willing to sacrifice your son?" I can imagine Abraham arguing with his voice within him, saying, "But he's my only son, and God promised that through my seed He would establish a great nation." I can imagine Abraham saying, "But I can't; I love him." And I can imagine Abraham deciding that if this was God's command, he must obey no matter what the cost. Maybe he was not quite sure even when he started on the journey. Maybe he thought, "The only way I can find out is to try it, to go step by step, and see how far He leads me."

Again it is possible that this came to him, as so many commands of God did, in a dream, and that the dream did not really mean that he should kill Isaac, but that Isaac should represent all that he held most dear; that the dream really asked him whether he would be willing to give up anything that God demanded. I do not know. And yet within my own heart I feel quite sure that God never intended for Abraham to sacrifice his son Isaac. Indeed, He could not. It would be utterly impossible, for that would be murder, contrary to the very laws of God.

Abraham, however, went forth and obeyed, and he would have done this wicked thing if God had not provided an angel who commanded him to stop, and a ram caught in the bushes which he sacrificed in place of his son Isaac. And God looked upon his obedience, and counted it to him as righteousness.

When I was in Australia I heard this wonderful story. Missionaries in the Outback were attacked by Aborigines on horseback. Helpless, they stood and waited to be killed, but the horses suddenly reared in terror and ran away! Later, when the Aborigines were converted, the missionaries inquired of this matter. "Did you not see the shining ones?" said the chief. "The horses saw them first, and then we saw them, and we were much afraid."

Apparently spiritual beings can manifest themselves either in light, or in a body of light, or in a body of flesh, according to the will of God whose messengers they are. Understand it I may not, but believe it I must! It has happened too often.

Are we really supposed to believe, then, that Abraham saw an angel and heard his voice? (Gen. 22:11-12) During the age of rationalism from which by the grace of God we are now beginning to emerge, it was unfashionable to believe that people can see angels. But actually I am quite sure that more people see angels today than did in Abraham's day, and I could fill many chapters with stories about them.

For instance, a retired missionary to Africa, Leslie Sutton, told me this story during a conference in Lee Abbey, England. His houseboy ran to him one day in excitement saying, "The Great One is coming up the hill with all his men!" The African chieftan was not a Christian, nor was he friendly with the British in Africa. Nevertheless the little missionary (for he was indeed small compared with the great African) went forth to meet him. There he came, glorious in his robes and feathers, and with him came many men. Two of them carried a chair; they set it down and the Great One established himself therein. Then he spoke to the missionary in words somewhat like these: "Last night I saw shining ones. They came down, they went up, they came down. In my hut I have a cockatoo; they had wings like my cockatoo. One of them said to me, 'Go and see the white man on the hill, because he has the words of God.' So I am here. Speak!" The missionary spoke, and many believed him because of their chieftain who had seen in his spirit the realities of God.

This is an old story, but I will now tell you a new one, only in fact some three weeks old. A child was playing with the handle of a car door as his mother drove on a California freeway. The door flew open, and the child rolled across three lanes of traffic, all traveling at high speed. Every car stopped; no car was hurt; the child was not hurt. If you know the freeways of the Los Angeles area, you will know that this was a miracle. When the mother picked the child up, he said, "Oh mother, did you see them?"

"See whom?" asked the mother.

"All the angels that stopped the traffic!"

There is an area of truth in this world that is visible not to the eyes of the flesh, nor to so-called rational seeing, but to the eyes of the spirit. This spiritual world is true, and the beings who live therein are real. The world of our own physical seeing some day will be no more, but God's kingdom of heaven, wherein dwell His messengers, is everlasting.

Therefore I believe without any question that when the Bible says that Abraham saw angels, Abraham saw angels.

Let us now consider one more of the incidents wherein Abraham saw angelic beings and was warned by them. We are told that three men appeared to Abraham, and these evidently were not men of this earth. (Gen. 18:2ff.) They were God's messengers; they were spiritual beings, but they were in the form of men. Abraham ran and hasted and rushed out to the field, and got a young calf and prepared supper for the men. Finally the men told him that God was going to do a great and terrible thing, that He was going to utterly destroy the city of Sodom because the wickedness of the people in that city had passed beyond measure.

God is a destroyer as well as a creator—or I should say, being a creator, God necessarily has the power and authority to destroy. It is not possible to be a creator unless one has this power and authority. I could not write a book unless I had the power and authority to take out certain pages of that book and throw them away, to scratch out certain words and destroy them utterly. No one can run a factory or make a dress or even cook a meal without having certain waste materials that must in some manner be changed or destroyed.

So therefore, being a good creator, God felt that it was necessary that the city of Sodom, whose wickedness had exceeded all imagination, should be destroyed from off the face of the earth. Putting the Scripture record of God's conversation with Abraham (Gen. 18:17ff.) into words that we might use, God said, "Shall I do anything without telling my friend Abraham?" So Abraham was told. Now follows that perfectly delightful story of Abraham "talking price" with God, as the Chinese would say, bargaining with God, reasoning with God.

Abraham said, "Would you destroy the righteous along with the wicked? You can't do a thing like that." And he said, "If there can be found fifty righteous people in this city, will you save it for the sake of the fifty?"

God said to him, "Yes, I will save the city if fifty righteous men can be found."

But there were not fifty, and so Abraham again reasoned with God and said, "If there can be found thirty, will you save it for the sake of thirty?"

And God replied, "Yes, I will."

But there were not thirty, and so the bargaining went on until at last Abraham said, "Oh, forgive me, Lord, if I speak just once more. If there can be found ten, will you save it for the sake of ten?"

And God said He would save it for the sake of ten.

But there could not be found ten; there could be found only three.

This is a perfectly reasonable story. Only three people could not, even with their combined faith, make a wide enough channel for God's power to come through for the saving of the city. I understand this manner of praying that Abraham entered into when he bargained with God. Those who listen to God are sometimes warned of impending danger or disaster and, being warned, they ask God, "May I pray for this to be averted?"

Sometimes the answer comes, "Yes, that is why I told you; that is why you are warned, so that you can pray for it to be averted." Sometimes, on the other hand, the answer comes to them, "No, this must happen," for one reason or another.

Then one thinks, "Well, Lord, may I pray for it to be lessened, for the destructive power of it to be reduced?"

Sometimes the answer is, "Yes, pray." And again, the answer might be, "No, you cannot. There is not a wide enough channel of faith and righteousness in that part of the country; you cannot do it." In such a case as this, one can only pray for those whom one knows and loves in that section to be saved out of that disaster.

This I know from my own experience. I once had a premonition of some disaster, probably an earthquake, coming to a certain section of this country, and I thought, "May I pray for it to be averted?"

And the answer came, "No, it cannot be averted; it must take place." I do not know, of course, whether that was because of any wickedness of the people therein, or simply because of the natural laws, the tension within the mountains that had to be released. At any rate that was it; it must take place. And so I prayed for it to quiet down, for the earth to quake without any loss of life, and with as little damage to property as possible. And so it was.

One can never prove, of course, whether these things are really answers to prayer, or whether they would have happened anyway. But if one has enough faith to pray for a certain thing, and then it happens, one should in all honesty at least consider the possibility that it was an answer to prayer. Not to believe this would be denying the very faith that caused one to pray.

So I understand this prayer of Abraham's concerning Sodom, the city of Lot. We are told that two angels entered the city at evening in the form of men. (Gen. 19:1ff.) These men led Lot and his wife and family out of the city before calamity fell. God rained fire and brimstone upon the city from heaven. Perhaps the fire and brimstone came from a volcanic eruption. Perhaps there was some other kind of explosion from the earth or one of the heavenly bodies. I do not know. But the city was destroyed, completely destroyed, and Lot's wife who lingered and did not run with all speed to get away from it was killed by her lingering. She became a "pillar of salt." (Gen. 19:26) Some kind of chemical released by this calamity apparently solidified her body and encrusted it with salt, so that it was later found like a mummy.

Now let us consider another fact concerning Abraham. This great mystic was a tycoon. He was a big businessman. We was a man of tremendous wealth. God blessed him with cattle and with gold and with silver, and multiplied him exceedingly, so that the man Abraham was very rich.

This may startle some of us. Somehow we have absorbed the idea that a mystic must be one who gives up all wealth and all material advantage and power, and lives a life of poverty. At this point we are apt to remember the story of the rich young ruler to whom Jesus said, "If thou wilt be perfect, go and sell that thou hast, and give to the poor, and thou shalt have treasure in heaven: and come and follow me." (Matt. 19:21) How then can we account for the fact that Abraham, the friend of God, was, on the other hand, never told to sell all that he had, but was continually blessed and increased and multiplied in his business?

Actually the explanation is very simple! People are

different. God did not make people after the same pattern. There is no such thing as standardization in the heavenly kingdom. The human concept of all men being created equal is laughable in the face of the teachings of the Bible. They are equal in the sense that they all deserve consideration. They are all entitled to life, liberty, and the pursuit of happiness. One might say, therefore, that in the eyes of the justice of the law they are equal. But that is the only way in which they are equal. Their talents vary. Their gifts vary. And the plans that God has for their lives on earth vary exceedingly!

When the rich young ruler came to Jesus, Jesus looked upon him and loved him. (Mark 10:21) He felt toward him a real, outgoing, outrushing flow of genuine affection, and I believe that when He told him to go and sell all that he had and give to the poor, and to come and follow Him, He meant exactly what He said. I believe He was inviting this man to become one of His disciples. If this rich young ruler had accepted the invitation, we would for a brief time have had thirteen disciples, not twelve, and when Judas failed and dropped out of that little band, we would have had the twelve originally planned. If the young man, therefore, was to become one of Jesus' followers, it was obviously necessary that he separate himself from the responsibilities of his business.

There are some people today, I am quite sure, who are created for this very thing. There are those called to give up everything, and to live and serve God through constant prayer and worship in a monastery or convent. We admire these holy ones with all our hearts. The power that they generate is beyond anything that we can know.

Abraham however was not called to the cloistered life. His gifts differed. The Holy Spirit gave Abraham a gift of government, a gift of organization, administration, business acumen. We are mistaken if we limit the gifts of the Holy Spirit to those in 1 Corinthians 12:8-10. Other verses at the end of that same chapter add gifts of teaching, preaching, helps, and government. Nor is this meant to be an exclusive list. The Holy Spirit is simply God's life abiding in us, and that life of God abiding in us explodes and increases and sets in motion whatever gifts are part of our natural personality and being.

Abraham was a "ten-talent man," having gifts of administration, of running a successful business. Abraham honored God through the running of his business. The laws of God as they operated in Abraham's life were not laws of poverty, but laws of abundance and prosperity. This was by the direct will of God (Gen. 17:6-8), and was also in answer to Abraham's faith. (Gen. 22:16-18)

Many of us were brought up with the idea that it is wrong to desire money, and unthinkable to pray concerning money. The story of Abraham should heal us of this poverty complex. Let us rethink that matter of God and money.

First, when we pray for money, let us remind ourselves that all the money in the world is in God's hands. All the cattle on a thousand hills are His. (Ps. 50:10) All the supply, all the produce, is in His hands, and is in mysterious ways under His control. He can order and direct it through the minds of men, or through miracles of nature, or in other ways that we know not, but He has complete power over His own abundance.

Once in Texas a Negro friend of mine, Mrs. Alice Smothers, told me about the children's home that she built. All the money for it was provided by God through the minds of men. A white lady once came to visit her school, and as she looked about she said, "Why, this is beautiful! This looks like a place where rich white children might live!" And Mrs. Smothers said to her, "These children are very rich; God is their Father, and He is the richest one of all."

God is our Father, and He is the richest one of all. Since God is our Father, therefore we are His heirs, as St. Paul told us in the eighth chapter of the Epistle to the Romans. We are "heirs of God, and joint-heirs with Christ." (Rom. 8:17) Therefore we have a right to ask God with an open mind and a believing heart for whatever we need of money and supply.

As we ask Him, we follow the same laws of faith that we follow in every other kind of praying. That is, we believe that He is giving us this supply that we need, and we imagine it flowing toward us. We "see" it coming to us by checks in the mail, by offers of business given on the telephone, by doors opening in response to someone's suggestion or from reading the advertisements in the paper, or in whatever way God knows to be best.

This last thought is very important. Prayer for the healing of the bank account does not usually work if we direct and outline the way in which God shall answer it. It is not wise to say, "Oh God, please make So-and-So raise my salary, or please make So-and-So pay what he owes me, or please inspire this rich person to give me a gift." Our prayer is more apt to be answered if we leave the door open, trusting God.

I could tell you many, many stories of money coming in ways utterly unexpected. A minister told me that one of his parishioners came to him in great distress, having immediate need of $5,000 to save his business. The minister had no money, of course, but he prayed with the parishioner that this need would be supplied. That very day a woman to whom he had ministered thirty-five years before called him from a distant city and said, "God just told me to send you a check for $5,000. This is not for your church; it is for you to use in whatever way you desire." You see, God is not limited! Needless to say, the minister loaned the man the $5,000; the business was saved, and in course of time the money was returned so that the minister could use it in other constructive ways.

Let us now consider the next point. Yes, we have a right to ask God for money, because He is our Father. But on the other hand, we do not even belong to ourselves. We are bought with a price. We belong to Jesus

Christ. Therefore we have no right to anything merely to have it and hold it, or to waste it foolishly, but only to use it as He directs us. Our next responsibility, therefore, is to use whatever money comes to us with wisdom and honesty, common sense and guidance.

Let us again consider Abraham. Abraham met Melchizedek, the king of Salem (Gen. 14:17ff.) who was priest as well as king, and gave him a tithe of all that he possessed. (Gen. 14:20) From that day to this, right down through the Bible, we are told that a tenth is a natural and rightful amount to give to God. (In those days, of course, the giving of the tenth to the priest included not only what would be used in the temple worship itself, but also what we could call charities.)

There is magic in this giving of a tithe. God manifests Himself not only in dreams and visions, but He manifests Himself in the way that His power works through money and business, and in all such practical matters.

The lessons drawn from the study of Abraham have usually been lessons in faith and obedience. These are rather obvious. But I delight in finding in this patriarch of all patriarchs lessons also in the relationship between God and man's possessions, expressed in Abraham's day in terms of cattle and sheep and he-asses and she-asses, and in our day less quaintly in terms of money.

More than all else I delight in finding here a key to the taking of that dominion over the earth that God gave to Adam, the dominion for which the earth is waiting. "For the earnest expectation of the creature waiteth for the manifestation of the sons of God." (Rom. 8:19) If there had been more righteous ones available in the cities of Sodom and Gomorrah, the earth would not have been devastated by fire and brimstone. The plains round about would not have been so bitterly laid waste that a body left therein was turned to a pillar of salt. The little animals that lived there would not have perished in a fiery death.

God has power to heal not only individuals but

also the earth itself. The sins of man have caused God's pleasant pastures to be burned into a desolate wilderness, as Jeremiah said. (Jer. 12:10-11) The righteousness of a few may serve as a channel of God's forgiving power, if there be but one able to stand before God as His friend and to plead for the land and for the cities, that they may be saved.

The anthropologist-priest Pierre Teilhard de Chardin is becoming more and more recognized as the greatest religious thinker of his age. Let us hear what he says upon this matter, in *The Hymn of the Universe*, "Pensees," section 70:

> To read the gospel with an open mind is to see beyond all possibility of doubt that Jesus came to bring us new truths concerning our destiny: not only a new life superior to that we are conscious of, but also in a very real sense a new physical power of acting upon our *temporal* world.
>
> Through a failure to grasp the exact nature of this power newly bestowed on all who put their confidence in God . . . many Christians neglect this earthly aspect of the promises of the Master, or at least do not give themselves to it with that complete hardihood which he nevertheless never tires of asking of us, if only we have ears to hear him.
>
> We must not allow timidity or modesty to turn us into poor craftsmen. If it is true that the development of the world can be influenced by our faith in Christ, then to let this power lie dormant within us would indeed be unpardonable.

6
Moses

✳

Moses was not a holy man—not in the beginning. God might have chosen as His messenger at that time a hermit or a mystic hiding within a cave and meditating on ethereal things, but He did not. The qualities He needed were wisdom and a fiery courage. Moses was a violent man. The story of his adult life begins with murder, although an excusable murder, if there be such a thing. He saw an Egyptian beating an Israelite. He had been abandoned in infancy, because of Pharaoh's orders that all male children of the Hebrews should be destroyed. His mother, with true Israelite shrewdness, had placed him in a waterproof basket among the bulrushes at the river where Pharaoh's daughter went to bathe. The princess found him and adopted him, and the mother became his wet-nurse. (Exod. 2:1-10)

Moses was brought up, therefore, as an Egyptian prince versed in all the occult wisdom of that ancient race. But in time of crises, Moses knew that he was an Israelite and rushed to the defense of his brothers.

After he killed the Egyptian he ran away from the wrath of Pharaoh and lived for many years as a sheepherder in the desert. Here it was that God called him. At first Moses could not hear God's voice, for the ears of his heart were dimmed. If he did feel a strange disturbance, and think thoughts that were not quite his own, he no doubt tried to forget them, just as many a person does today. But God made His light so visible that Moses could not help but see it. It shone within a bush like fire, and yet the bush was not destroyed. "And Moses said, I will now turn aside and see this great sight, why the bush is not burnt." (Exod. 3:1-3)

It is no problem to me to believe that Moses saw a light or fire not of this earth. I have seen a bit of this myself, and so have countless other people. Sometimes sensitive film can catch it, when the eye cannot. Indeed I have a snapshot of such a light upon the bare altar of a little chapel in Australia, taken after one of the Schools of Pastoral Care. There was no flashlight on the camera, no electric light in the chapel, and no sun shining through the clouded sky. Some see this picture and do not believe it, but how can one explain scientifically the bright ball of light that appears on the altar? Moses did not believe it either and he watched to see the light change to a real fire and burn the bush. Then he heard the voice of God. (Exod. 3:4ff.) God called him to go to Pharaoh and demand that he set free his people.

Moses protested quite a bit, as many a minister has at first protested when receiving a similar call; and I know several who have first of all seen a light, and thus been electrified into attention. But Moses went! Read it in Exodus, Chapter 3ff. It is fascinating!

Fascinating but unbelievable, you are thinking— for instance, the magicians of Egypt making rods turn into snakes and back to rods. I do not understand it, but I have heard that mystics of the East do tricks such as making ropes come down from the sky, and climbing up those ropes. Do you believe this? I am not sure that I do, but there are those who do believe it and who say that there is a fourth dimension that from time to time breaks into our three-dimensional world and does strange things. I do not understand this and I am myself unable to figure out even the simplest conjuring trick. But it is interesting that people of all sorts are dreaming about the mysteries of life. What do you think about "Time Tunnel," "Twilight Zone," and all manner of science fiction? They prove nothing, of course, except one tremendous thing: that the heart of man is getting "cabin fever" here on the earth and longs to see farther and to hear more. And who knows how much more there is to see and hear? Many of us have had experiences that we do not tell lest people think us crazy, yet our common speech reflects them. For instance, we say that a thing has been "spirited away," when it has simply disappeared, we do not know how. We say that something "materializes" when it appears and no one knows from whence it came.

So—the Egyptian magicians knew tricks that I do not understand nor want to understand, for such knowledge would be too dangerous for me, as it was for Adam and Eve. Moses, growing up in the court of Pharaoh, was conversant with these mysteries, and by the direct action of God was given greater occult power than the Egyptians knew, and therefore was able in the presence of Pharaoh to confound them with their own tricks. So Pharaoh, being frightened, said that he would let the people of Israel go free. But in the morning he changed his mind.

Then there follows the most baffling and mysterious of all the miracles recounted in the Bible: the plagues of Egypt. We are told that the waters of the sea turned red, that the fish in the sea died, that there came a plague of frogs, a plague of lice, a plague of flies, murrain upon the cattle, locust, thunder and hail, three-day darkness, death within every Egyptian home. We are told also that each time there was a plague Pharaoh promised to let the people go, and each time God hardened Pharaoh's heart so that he changed his mind and the plagues went on. (Exod. 9:12,35, etc.)

The perplexing thing is not that God might bring forth such miracles of destruction, for certainly He can, and such plagues happen today. I have seen in China a plague of locusts covering the earth. Sandstorms are known in the great desert to darken the sun for days so that no one can go out of house or tent. Seas have been poisoned so that fish have died on their shores. Industrial waste poisons some of our own waters. But what could have poisoned the Red Sea and started a chain of plagues?

I have heard one theory, strange and yet to me believable: that it was the red dust of atomic fallout that poisoned the sea, making it corrupt like blood so that no life could remain in it. Where this could have come from, if indeed it did come, I do not know. Was there some volcano, since covered with the shifting sands of the desert? Was there some heavenly body that exploded with a rain of atomic dust, as heavenly bodies do at times explode? Who can tell? But I do not put it past the power of the Creator, who is also a destroyer, to bring about such a thing. And if the seas were poisoned, that alone could bring swarms of frogs and lice and flies and even locusts to feed upon the pollution, scavengers as they are. Nor does it puzzle me that with such corruption loose upon the land of Egypt there might be sores (atomic burns?) upon man and beast, followed by death. Nor am I unable to believe that God could by a miracle surround His own people with protection, so that the destruction did not come nigh them.

But what I do not understand is: *why?* Did Moses hear God correctly when he concluded that it was by the will of God that Pharaoh hardened his heart so that more destruction was necessary to bring him into subjection? Or did some great catastrophe actually happen at that time, and did Moses figure that its train of succeeding circumstances were all independently willed by God to spite Pharaoh?

Possibly some of you are shocked at this point, thinking, "But you are questioning the words of the Bible!" Well, Jesus did. "Ye have heard that it was said by them of old time" (Matt. 5:21, 27, 33, etc.) By whom? By Moses. "Ye have heard that it hath been said, an eye for an eye, and a tooth for a tooth: but I say unto you, that ye resist not evil." (Matt. 5:38-39) Jesus retranslated the nature of God and the will of God. And to make a right estimate of the Creator, surely we may consider not only what Moses said, according to the best of his knowledge, but also what Jesus said in His farther reach of understanding.

However, I am not retranslating. I merely say that I do not know. When I get to heaven, I will ask Him: "Lord, what did you mean by all those plagues of Egypt?" But in the meantime I believe, first, that these calamities did happen to Egypt and, second, that God used them in some way to disturb Pharaoh so that the king at last decided that the people of Israel were bad luck to him, and had better let them go.

Off they went, therefore, taking with them earrings of gold and jewels of gold that they borrowed from the Egyptians and were conveniently unable to return. (Exod. 12:35-36) They felt that this was right, doubtless, since the Egyptians owed them a great deal. Was it? I wonder.

Anyway, off they went, and Pharaoh changed his mind again. (Perhaps his wife complained about her earrings!) He pursued them and caught up with them on the banks of the Red Sea. And the Lord said unto Moses, as he faced his people's panic and anger, "Wherefore criest thou unto me? Speak unto the children of Israel, that they go forward." (Exod. 14:15) With the sea before them, and the desert on either side, and Pharaoh's chariots behind them!

But they went. And the Lord did strange things. The pillar of cloud and fire with which He led them moved and stood behind them and was to the Egyptians darkness, but to the Israelites it gave light, as it was wont to do when it led them through the wilderness at night. (Exod. 13:21; 14:19-20) Do you believe this? If you have never seen the light of God, then I do not blame you if you cannot believe it. But when you have seen even a little bit of that light, it is not quite so difficult to think that God could send them a pillar of fire that shone by night to guide them. Moreover, the Lord made a strong east wind to blow all night (Exod. 14:21) so that the waters in this narrow crossing were blown away and were like a wall of protection to the people. (This, I have been told, does happen from time to time in that shallow part of the Red Sea.) And the Israelites went over, as though walking on dry land. But the armies of Pharaoh, venturing into the sea the next day, were caught in the returning waters, and their chariots drove heavily and their wheels were stuck in the mud. The waters rose more and more, and Pharaoh and his armies were "drowned in the Red, Red Sea," as we sing to this day. (Exod. 14:28) But the wives and children of the Egyptians did not sing. From the vantage point of so much time, we wonder why Jehovah showed such favoritism as to save the children of Israel and drown all the Egyptian soldiers.

Did he? After all, the Egyptians had free will. He did not force them to try that dangerous crossing. They could see that the strong east wind had died down. They could know that in the course of nature the waters would come back. They could figure out that chariot wheels would be likely to sink into the muddy bottom of the river. If they had been willing to listen to their own wisdom, surely God would not have tricked them. And if they had listened to God, surely they would have heard Him saying, "Better not try it!" Why, with all their occult wisdom, could they not hear the voice of God? For the same reason that those who experiment today with magic and soothsayers and ouija boards do not necessarily hear the voice of God. They are connecting with the wrong station. You do not hear Lawrence Welk if you tune in to "Gunsmoke" or "Lassie." Listening to one station across the air does not enable you to hear another station; in fact, it makes it more difficult. And you would not dream of listening to four or five different stations at once, for you would know that in the confusion you would hear nothing at all.

People often say, "What difference does it make whom you *call* God and whether you believe in Him through Jesus Christ, or through Buddha, or Baal, or the golden calf, or the holy cat of Bubastes? It's the same God." God is the same, yes, but not all stations lead to Him, any more than all television stations lead to Lawrence Welk. God is the same, yes, but not every road goes up His holy hill, any more than all roads in the United States lead to Mount Rainier.

Maybe some of Pharaoh's magicians inquired of their gods concerning the crossing of the Red Sea, but if so, the answer they received was not a true one, because the one with whom they connected was not the Lord Jehovah. The one who spoke to them might even have been Satan, the old enemy, still loose upon the earth, and past master of deception.

I am afraid, however, that the children of Israel did not worry about the Egyptian widows and orphans any more than we seem to worry about the widows and orphans of North Vietnam. They only rejoiced that the Lord had saved them, which of course He had. We are told moreover that Miriam, the older sister of Moses, did a song and dance of victory (Exod. 15:20-21), and all the children of Israel started across the desert with great joy.

It would take many pages to consider all the wanderings of the children of Israel through the desert. But the point of the intrepid Creator's whole venture seems to have been this: to reveal His laws to a people capable of obeying and teaching them, so that whether or not man heard His voice, they would at least know the laws according to which their natures were made, and could keep those laws, and therefore live in His light. In order to do this, God needed a very direct connection with man, so that man could read Him loud and clear. He needed, moreover, a somewhat dramatic way of making this revelation, so that the children of Israel would heed and believe and tremble and obey.

So He really put on a show! He warned Moses beforehand that He would descend upon Mount Sinai in a terrifying manner, and that no one, man or beast, was to come near or they would be put to death. (Exod. 19:10-13) This ferocity of God's used to trouble me greatly. But it has finally occurred to me that possibly the mountain was radioactive or in some way dangerous. Perhaps it was full of electricity, like a live wire. "And Mount Sinai was altogether on a smoke," so we read in Exodus 19:18, "because the Lord descended upon it in fire: and the smoke thereof ascended as the smoke of a furnace, and the whole mount quaked greatly." It sounds like a volcanic eruption and an earthquake, does it not? And it might have been that, among other things. However, whatever it was from a scientific point of view, it was too hot to handle; it was dangerous. And only Moses, who was divinely protected because of his nearness to God, was able to ascend and stay there safely. The Lord said unto him, "Thou shalt come up, thou, and Aaron with thee." (Exod. 19:24) But apparently Aaron "chickened out," for instead of ascending the mountain he stayed below and got himself and the children of Israel into trouble, bad trouble. (Exod. 32:1ff.)

Meanwhile there was given to Moses on the mount the most tremendous outpouring of the direct power of God that has ever been known upon the solid earth. We know that God's light is in all the earth, the very world itself being made of the radiation of His being. But God drew together, as it were, and directed toward the mountain a sunburst, an atomic explosion, of His being. The mountain smoked and rocked with it. The mind and spirit of Moses were caught up into it, so that for days on end he lived not in his physical body but in his spiritual body. We have two bodies, remember, the one physical, the other spiritual. We are usually aware only of the physical body and of the mind that directs it. But sometimes man is caught up into a larger awareness. The soul of man craves this larger awareness, knowing it as his birthright. Hence the wistful and dangerous experiments with hallucinatory drugs, which project one into a visionary state for which he is not prepared, and which therefore can unhinge the mind.

Moses did not need anything like LSD! He did not even need food or drink. He was living so intensely in the spirit that his body did not speak to him at all. In this high state of consciousness he heard the voice of God as a man hears another man speaking face to face. And from God he received the plan for a theocracy, a nation whose leader is God, the kind of nation that we must have upon this earth in order that the kingdom of heaven may come.

That and nothing else was Moses' tremendous job: to create a nation out of a mob of slaves, and to create it after the image and likeness of the kingdom of heaven, insofar as man was then able to attain that kingdom. He worked out, therefore, with God's direct inspiration, the moral code which we still read in our churches. He worked out also an intricate system of law and government, which in spite of its crudeness, and the harshess of the times in which it must function, is still the foundation of the government of two great nations, Great Britain and the United States. We call this the Mosaic Law. Moreover, God gave him an amazing system of hygiene and sanitation, and even of quarantine and the fumigation of houses wherein there had been infectious diseases. We must remember that this system was based on a world without refrigerators. The Israelites were forbidden to eat pork, for instance; it was unholy. So it is, for we know nowadays that pork, if not kept perfectly refrigerated and thoroughly cooked, causes trichinosis.

Meanwhile, as the mountain shook and flamed, and the children of Israel went on the rampage below it, God gave to Moses also an intricate and elaborate plan for erecting and decorating a tabernacle in which the glory of God could dwell in the wilderness. (Exod. 25ff.) As someone said, the Holy Spirit asked to be institutionalized! Why? Was it really to important to have a tabernacle, a sort of movable church, hung with purple and blue, and beautified with gold? Was it really necessary that the priests' robes be embroidered with gold and crimson and decorated with bells and pomegranates, and the surplices should be of fine twined linen, elaborately smocked? "God is a spirit," Jesus said, "and they that worship him must worship him in spirit and in truth." (John 4:24) Then why all the bells and embroidery?

To worship Him in spirit is to make contact with Him in spirit—to *see* Him. There have been those who have seen visions of His light in the heavens. All through the Bible, and all though the history of the saints, and down to the present day there have been those who in the midst of this distressful life have been caught up into an awareness of the world of God.

I remember the first time this happened to me. I was in a bad mood; my children were sick; the house was a mess; and I climbed thunderously into the car to fetch my friend and helper, Elizabeth. As I drove through the frosty late winter countryside, all of a sudden everything changed—and yet it was the same. I saw the pale earth-shine of the early moon in the sky, and I was part of the moon and knew the feeling of moonness. I was part of the pinpoints of winter wheat pushing through melting snow. I was part of the peach tree whose twigs were beginning to glow with uprising sap. I could feel the sap pushing its way into life. The pulse of God and His world was in my pulse. In that instance I worshipped God in spirit and in truth.

One cannot always capture the sheer givenness of moments like this. However, walking solidly upon this earth there is another way of glimpsing the glory of God, and that is in the holy hush of a church lit purple and red by its stained-glass windows, hung with fine twined linen upon its altar, brightened with shining vases and embroidered hangings. Why does all this beauty comfort and still my soul? Is it simply the appeal of beauty and order? Or is it that this reflects in some faint way the beauty and order of that heavenly kingdom from which the soul has come, and therefore fills the unconscious being with wistful memories and with the unreasonable reassurance of a life that is from everlasting? I do not know, but so it is.

It is true, as many people say, that God is everywhere and that one should be able to worship Him in spirit and truth on the freeway, or in the kitchen, or beside the sea. But I myself am not able to see Him in all places. On the freeway, and in my kitchen, and even beside the sea there is too much to remind me of this earth. My spirit cannot rise to merge with His Spirit, which merging is true worship. Some claim to find God on the golf course of a Sunday morning but being by nature a doubting Thomas, I cannot really believe that they are looking for a burning bush behind every tree. Sometimes it may be that a glimpse of eternal glory shines through a tall tree into their minds. Sometimes beside the sea my spirit leaves this earth and floats upon ethereal waves into the light of God. But I cannot bid it do so.

When I go to church, however, to a church that believes in the symbolism of beauty and strives for it, and most of all to a church that adores the beauty of Jesus, I find it much easier to forget the world and to sense within me the peace and joy and awakening love of heaven. Therefore I am able to imagine that the plan for the tabernacle came from God with a real purpose behind it: the purifying and enlightening of the people.

But the light faded upon the mountain, the smoke died away, and the quaking ceased, and Moses descended again to the plain, as we all have to descend after a while. This moment of descent is the most dangerous of all. We may have forgotten that an enemy is still rampant upon the earth, disguising himself in every kind of holy disguise in order to fool us. His greatest trick, of course, is to convince us that there is not really any Satan, and that if we are truly civilized and enlightened we will know that Satan is merely the dark side of our own souls, and that knowing this has in itself healing value. Thus he endeavors to persuade us that good is evil and evil good, and as soon as we accept that theory we are finished, and Satan laughs at us and says to God, "You see, I told you so!"

While Moses was on the mountain Satan had persuaded the Israelites that evil was good, and there was no difference really, and that the golden calf which the Egyptians worshiped was a symbol of God, and more practical than the dreams and visions of Moses, who seemed in any case to have completely disappeared. (Exod. 32)

Aaron, the high priest, Moses' brother, gathered from the people the earrings and ornaments of gold that they had borrowed from the Egyptians. (Presumably if they had not thought that God told them to take these ornaments, there would have been no golden calf.) He melted them down and fashioned an idol in the shape of a calf, and in the place of God they worshipped it with dancing and singing, working themselves into a fine frenzy and snatching off their clothes and acting in lewd fashion the better to experience "reality." This met Moses' eyes as he came down from the mountain, doubtless expecting the Israelites to be awaiting him upon their knees. And in the fury of sudden reaction he dropped or flung down the tablets of stone on which he had with the finger of God written the ten commandments, and they broke. (Exod. 32:19)

We should not be too surprised, for in a small way this kind of thing has happened to us. The Bible is most miraculously not only a rip-roaring history of a turbulent people, but also a mirror of our own souls. I have come back to the rectory after a three-hour service to find the children dancing around the house messing up everything, the coffeepot boiling over on the stove, and the toilet stopped up because someone threw a teddy bear in it, and I have flung down the ten commandments that God wrote in my heart and have smacked people left and right. Maybe they deserved it, but my ten commandments were broken.

Someone said, "But I can't believe that Moses came down from the mountain lugging two huge engraved tombstones decorated with scrolls." Of course he didn't! That idea did not come from the Bible, but probably from an exuberant artist illustrating a Sunday school book. Moses did not have a notebook on that mountain, nor a ballpoint pen. But the most essential part of his whole revelation from God he wanted to keep, word for word. Where would it be inscribed but on stone? I have seen natural layers of rock a sixteenth of an inch thick, and I can imagine God not only giving Moses the revelation of the ten commandments, but somehow helping him to scratch them upon these fragments of slatelike rock. And they were broken. But that was not such a great matter, for Moses remembered them, and with the help of God could write them again.

The great matter was that Moses' heart was broken, and in the fury of his reaction he visited a terrible punishment upon his own people. Why was his heart broken? What was so awful, really, about worshiping some kind of god represented by a golden calf? It didn't have to go on forever; the people could put on their clothes again and quiet down and behave themselves.

Yes, but they had made a connection between their souls and the devil, and it is not so easy to break that connection, for the devil is loath to let go of the power he has put upon a person. This I know of a certainty. I have prayed for release for too many people in the grip of the enemy not to know it. It takes all my strength to channel God's power to free them. They are released, but what of the thousands who walk in darkness and do not know that there is any light way? What of those who feel that the festering evil within them is nothing but the shadow side of themselves, and that they must learn to live with it? What of those who tune in to wrong stations, until they actually become possessed and throw themselves off bridges because there is no point in living? What of the multitude who have taken a wrong path, one that will lead them into tribulation, as surely as the day leads into night? Moses hoped to forstall this when he purged the people. (Exod. 32:26-28) But he could not forestall it. The gossamer threads of an evil connection remained among the people, and cropped up again and again as the long histories of Kings and Chronicles make clear. Therefore God said to Moses, "Nevertheless in the day

when I visit I will visit their sin upon them." (Exod.
32:34) This was not a willful act of vengeance perpe-
trated by a furious Jehovah. It was simply the working
out of a law. God does not break His laws.

Moses had seen the blueprint of a nation whose God
is the Lord and who walk in the light and in the freedom of that light. In agony of soul he went to the most
desperate lengths to convince them of the danger and
the evil of idol worship, and to bring them back to
God. It grieves me to think of this purging of the people, as it grieves me to think of all the other "purges"
in the sad and violent history of our race. Now a better
way has been provided—the blood sacrifice of the Lamb
of God—but in that day His coming was so far away
that Moses did not see it through the tunnel of time.
Knowing the great and good heart of this giant among
men, I imagine that he carried the burden of this grief
until he laid it down atop a mountain of final depart-
ing. Indeed, it seems possible that this was the real
burden of guilt that lay upon him so heavily that he
did not feel capable of leading his people into the land
of Canaan. Perhaps he was so worn down by his strug-
gles with them that he could not endure any more.

Moses obviously could not have written the story of
his own death. Whoever wrote it evidently believed
that Moses' act of vengeance upon his people was right
and just, and that the only reason Moses was barred
from the land of Canaan was his striking the rock in
the wilderness of Zin. (Num. 20:7-13) We cannot help
wondering: did Moses' failure to sanctify God in the
midst of the children of Israel (Deut. 32:51) refer to
more than his striking the rock? It would seem to us
that his slaughter of three thousand of his brethren
was a greater sin. Was Moses himself unaware of this?
Or did he feel a burden of guilt, and yet deem it unwise to declare it? I wonder.

Now before we meditate upon the departure of this
prince among men, Moses, let us consider one of the
many puzzling incidents of his travel through the wilderness, leading the cantankerous children of Israel.

The Lord had given them a mysterious food that they called "manna" for lack of a better name. (Exod. 16:11ff.) I cannot explain this edible substance found upon the ground; nevertheless I believe it, for Jesus Himself spoke of it as real. (John 6:49) Maybe in some far day a scientist will discover it and so rejoice our hearts. But the Israelites got tired of "Manna" and complained against Moses. Then the Lord sent serpents who bit and killed many of them. (Num. 21:5-6)

Is there any sense in all this? There may be. It is natural for snakes to live in the wilderness; the Lord did not need to create those snakes in order for them to bite the Israelites. But when the people fell to complaining and fussing and feeling sorry for themselves, they laid themselves open to any danger that was around them. In such a state, when one sees a snake one fears it and the serpent is apt to feel the fear and attack. I believe and know that when one is filled with the love of God and has no fear, a serpent is not likely to harm him. J. Allen Boone's delightful book *Kinship with All Life* propounds this idea. A friend of mine who is part Indian says that snakes do not bite Indians because an Indian knows how to walk among them without fear. But when the mind is upset with anger and bitterness, then fear enters on the heels of guilt, and, seeing a snake, one expects to be bitten by it.

Moses prayed for the sick people, now repentant, that they might be healed. The Lord told him to make a snake of brass and set it upon a pole and let the people look to it and be healed. Moses did so, and they were healed. (Num. 21:7-9) They changed their point of view. They looked upon the very thing that had hurt them and believed that it was now turned into a source of healing, and so it was.

Herein is a most profound lesson. If we can look at the very thing that has plagued us, and believe that it can be turned into a source of healing, then it will be tool of power, a stepping-stone instead of a stumbling block. How often I have rejoiced because of my own years of depression. But for them I would not be able to help others who are distressed. I say to unhappy people, "Yes, I used to be that way, and the Lord healed me." Immediately the serpent of mental agony is redeemed and set up so that others can look at it and live.

Just as illness comes often from fear and guilt, so healing comes often from taking the guilt thing that made us afraid, lifting it up into the sunlight of God's love, and seeing it redeemed and turned to power. For many an illness is an illness of soul as well as of body: psychosomatic. (Doctors use this long word and thus make it valid!)

But how do we know that evil can be redeemed? Because Jesus Christ took it unto Himself and died upon the cross for it, and thus we are saved. "And as Moses lifted up the serpent in the wilderness, even so must the Son of man be lifted up: that whosoever believeth in him should not perish, but have eternal life." (John 3:14-15)

I believe this because it works. An alcoholic when lifted up into a new person can lift other alcoholics. One healed of physical illness can inspire in others the faith to be healed. Best of all, one can know that the most poisonous thing within us—our darkest secret and our most disgusting sin—can be transformed, lifted up, and made our greatest source of life and healing.

The life of Moses, this great man of God, ended when he was a hundred and twenty years old. "His eye was not dim, nor his natural force abated." (Deut. 34:7) Moreover, before he departed this life he gave his family, the children of Israel, the most beautiful farewell address ever given, unless it is Jesus' farewell address in John 14-17. Deuteronomy, Chapters 29-33 are glorious and stirring and full of power. Read them! You need not read all about the buildings of the temple, nor the numbering of the tribes, nor the laws of government, but these chapters are for you. Read them!

How did Moses know that he was going to depart this life? God told him, of course. (Deut. 31:2) But I use the words "depart this life" advisedly, for there is a mystery concerning the death of Moses. We are told that nobody ever saw his grave. (Deut. 34:6) We are told that Michael, the archangel, contended with the devil about the body of Moses. (Jude 9) Why? Could it be because God intended to send the spirit of Moses again into his body, so that he accomplished the resurrection of the body then and at that time, as Jesus later did, so that his body did not decay but walked with God, as Enoch did? (Gen. 5:24)

When Jesus was transfigured upon the mountaintop, there appeared with Him two men (Matt. 17:3), Moses and Elijah. Elijah ascended into heaven in an appearance like a chariot of fire. (2 Kings 2:11) And Moses departed with God up into the mountain alone, and no one ever saw him die nor ever saw his grave. (Deut. 34:1-6) Could it be then that God sent to be with Jesus those two who had already achieved their resurrection bodies—who did not die as other men have died? God never sent ghosts to speak to men. Summoning the spirits of the departed was the work of witches and wizards and was strictly forbidden all through the Bible. (E.g., Deut. 18:10-12) Elijah was not a ghost. He was a man living in his immortal body. And I love to think that to Moses also this great boon might have been given: that he did indeed lead his people into a promised land, a land not seen with the eyes of the body, but a land more real and beautiful than any land on earth.

7

Elijah and Elisha

✳

In the beginning there was direct communication between God and man. This direct communication was broken; man went against the guiding voice within him. From that time, on, the Creator sought for these lost children of His. He tried to show Himself to them through nature, as we have seen: a burning bush, pillars of cloud and of fire, a blazing and bursting theophany on top of Mount Sinai. As He thus showed forth His glory He chose certain great men and prophets to interpret Him to the people. One of these was Moses, possibly the greatest man of the Old Testament.

The miracles of Moses were initiated by God Himself. God lit the fire within the burning bush, and Moses looked upon it and wondered. God turned back the waters of the Red Sea, and brought water from the rock, and quail and manna out of the air that the children of Israel might eat and be satisfied. Moses merely stretched forth his rod or opened his mouth and spoke when God commanded him to do so. Indeed the Creator carried His children in His arms, except at such times as they scrambled out of His arms and ran away.

But His children grew up, as children do. And the time came when he set them down upon their feet and let them walk. He gave to certain chosen and great ones a gift of miracles, as He has apparently given this gift today to certain well-known evangelists. Elijah was enwrapped with the mantle of God's power and his pupil and helper Elisha inherited that power when Elijah went away from him.

Later on, after Jesus sent His Holy Spirit into the world, the picture changed again. In addition to some greatly filled with power, that same word of power is spoken by God to all men, and those who hear it and follow Him are inheritors of His creativity. (Heb. 1: 1-4) We do not have to run and find a Moses nor any special person if we seek God with all our hearts. We ourselves can learn to contact that flow of creativity that is His healing light still shining. We ourselves can reach out by our small humble prayer of faith and can connect our spirit with His great flow of the power that heals and works miracles upon the face of the earth. Concerning this I have written many books: *The Healing Light* with specific directions about learning and using the prayer of faith; *Oh, Watchman* and *Lost Shepherd,* amplifications and applications of this in narrative form; *Let's Believe,* the teaching of the prayer of faith to little children, and others. We can now do this because we do not work alone; Jesus Christ has mysteriously made Himself a part of mankind and His power is available to all of those who call upon His name.

Before He came, however, there were certain great miracle-workers and the greatest of these seem to me to be Elijah and Elisha. They themselves were in touch with higher energy than most men knew: the creativity of God. They themselves used this power according to their own wills. Usually they did works that Jesus would have done and indeed, that He did do later on: works of healing and helping, providing food for starving bodies and life for starving souls. Occasionally, however, they used this power in ways that surely Jesus would not have done. For instance, Elijah had infuriated King Ahab by preaching to him somewhat too vigorously. The king therefore, with due respect for the prophet's powers, sent fifty soldiers to arrest him. Whereupon Elijah called down fire from heaven to destroy them. (2 Kings 1:9-10) Whence the fire came and what means produced it—I do not know. But the point that baffles me is that when Elijah sent forth the word of power, the fire did come. Why did God permit this to be?

True, Elijah doubtless felt it quite necessary and permissible, as the United States felt it quite necessary and permissible to send down fire upon Hiroshima and Nagasaki and destroy men, women, and children, who were surely less menacing than Ahab's fifty soldiers. But we had to do that in order to end the war, we say. When I mention, knowing the Oriental people as I do, that we needed only to tell the Japanese what we intended doing and it would have not been necessary, people do not like it. Naturally. It gives us an unhappy guilt feeling. We would prefer to shroud our guilt feeling and push it under cover, whence it escapes in rebellion against all government. Nevertheless I know that this is true. Japan was asking for terms of surrender and we were insisting that it must be unconditional. But we did not understand the Japanese nor realize the wide swing of the Oriental nature between good and evil which I have mentioned before. We did not realize that they thought all people were thus and expected murder, torture, and rape as our price of victory. If only we had told them what our price was, we would not have needed to turn the course of the world toward destruction by using the atomic bomb.

If Elijah had only asked the soldiers, "What are you going to do to me?" he would not have needed to destroy them. They would have said, "Come on down. We aren't going to hurt you." Finally God Himself said to Elijah (presumably when the prophet remembered to ask Him), "Go down with him: be not afraid of him." (2 Kings 1:15) Very likely God had been shouting this into Elijah's inner ear for some time, but Elijah had been too frightened to listen.

But why did God permit Elijah to use His power so destructively? And why did he permit us to use His power destructively over Japan? True, it was a different kind of power. But both destructive energies were created by the Creator. Why then did He not keep them in His own hands and forbid man to use them?

It is the old question: Why did He give man free will? Why was the power of choice given to us who are obviously so incapable of always choosing correctly?

It is a common assumption that if we pray for something that would be destructive either to us or to someone else God will not answer the prayer. I find that an oversimplification. Sometimes indeed God answers the desires of our hearts (unconscious) rather than the desires of our minds. But at other times if we are determined to pray for something that we later regret, He still answers the prayer. I suppose it is a matter of putting His children down and letting them walk. Sometimes a father will pick up his child before he stumbles, but at other times he will let him learn by stumbling.

At any rate, God did not, so far as we know, reprove Elijah for his overenthusiastic calling down of heavenly fire, nor did He reprove Elisha when in a moment of exasperation he called for two bears to come out of the woods and "tear" the rude children who insulted him. (2 Kings 2: 23-24) I trust that the attack by the she-bears upon the fleeing children had not fatal results. Nevertheless, Jesus would not have done that.

But the Lord God knew that Jesus had not yet come and He did not hold it against these first among the miracle-workers that they used the power occasionally in ways that we, I hope, would not have done.

I come to this conclusion because to Elijah was given the greatest gift that man can have: to pass into immortal life without going through death. And to Elisha was given a gift almost as great: to see his master depart, body and all, into the heavens and to receive that "mantle" which was the symbol or the channel of Elijah's power. (2 Kings 2:9-14)

This is the first account of an unidentified flying object that I know of. Read it if you don't believe me! If a chariot of fire appearing in the sky and moving as by a whirlwind is not an unidentified flying object I do not know what it is! And the extraordinary prophet Elijah, alive and well and going on a long hike with his friend Elisha, was caught up in this thing drawn by an energy that the chronicler simply called "horses of fire" and was taken away, body and all, into the heavens and seen no more. Moreover he was told beforehand that the Lord would take him away this day. Indeed word of this coming event got around to many of the "sons of the prophets." They came and murmured it in Elisha's ear, and Elisha said, "Yeah, I know it. Be quiet!" Or in the words of the Bible, "Yea, I know it; hold ye your peace." (2 Kings 2:5)

These rip-roaring men of old moved in a whirlwind of spiritual energy and turned that energy into whatever the problems of life might be, whether they were fifty savage soldiers or an axhead that fell into the water and was lost. This sad event took place during the building of the first seminary (2 Kings 6:1-7) "Alas, master!" cried the unfortunate young man who had felled the beam so ferociously that the axhead fell into the water. "For it was borrowed!"

"Where'd you drop it?" said Elisha. The seminarian showed him. Whereupon the prophet cut a stick and cast it into the water and the axhead did swim: it came into sight and the young man put out his hand and took it.

I doubt very much whether an axhead would be retrieved in just this fashion if a seminarian were to drop it into a lake today and cry out to his professor, "Alas, master! It was borrowed!"

A professor of today would probably say that this story was a myth; that Elisha simply fished down with a stick and caught the axhead and drew it up. Maybe so. But I prefer to wonder whether the prophet did not call upon a miraculous power in order to make a thing heavier than water float on top of the water. We do this today with our steel ships. We call upon law of flotation, and indeed we call upon laws of speed and balance and weight so that even things heavier than air can fly within the air. What laws did Elisha call upon? I do not know.

What laws come into action when an unidentified flying object skips from horizon to horizon in a zigzag flight, something like a water-beetle on top of a lake, and all in a matter of seconds? I know that there are such things, for on one occasion I saw them. Not in a vision, I do assure you, and not in trance. Indeed, I was taking the garbage out to the garbage-can at eight o'clock on a bitter December night in New England, and I was never in a less mystical mood. Yet here they came over the top of the hill, balls apparently of fire burning low and flying like a whirlwind into the far sky. What were they? I do not know any more than I know whereof was made the chariot of fire which took up Elijah. (2 Kings 2:11) What caused them to move in that apparently irrational fashion contrary to all known laws of flight? I have no idea, any more than I have any idea what caused the axhead to float at least for a moment, so that it could be seized by the relieved hand of the overenthusiastic seminarian. Can one conceive of the energy of the Creator entering into the ax, dematerializing it—if I may use these words—transforming it into its spiritual essence, invisible and weightless, and then reforming it into a shape that could be seen on top of the water?

I have a friend who broke her hand in such a fashion that the doctor said it would be months before she could use it at all, and she would probably never get back its full use. I prayed for it with another friend, using the laying on of hands and praying in a pattern inspired by the story of the ax: that a spiritual power would enter the bones and melt them down into their spiritual essence and then reform them in the pattern of solid, uninjured bone. The next day her hand was perfect, a fact for which the doctor had no explanation.

Does this read like science fiction? Certainly it does. So does much of the two books of Kings: a miraculous power entering into oil so that it expanded in such a way that it filled every vessel in the house and saved a widow and her two sons from being sold into slavery for unpaid debts (2 Kings 4:1-7); entering into flour so that it proved inexhaustible and fed not only the prophet but also the widow and her family (1 Kings 17:8-16); God's power entering into salt so that when Elisha cast it into impure waters they were made pure (2 Kings 2:19-22); certainly it reads like science fiction!

However, these miracles are not nearly so remarkable as the miracles that we do today in purifying our water, and expanding an atom into a million times its natural size, and making usable objects of plastic out of the most impossible materials. "But we have learned how to use the laws of nature and do these things!" one may say. Surely. And in the years to come there will be other laws of God, the Creator of nature, that we will learn how to use, and things that we now do not believe will become commonplace knowledge. That is why I like to read science fiction, either in the Bible or out of it! For here and there I find mentioned an impossible miracle that man has begun to dream about and that will some day probably appear. Jules Verne wrote of submarines in his science-fiction book *Twenty Thousand Leagues under the Sea* many years before anyone dreamed that such a thing might be. Alfred Lord Tennyson saw a century and more ago "The heavens filled with commerce..." ("Locksley Hall") long before anyone ever dreamed of airplanes. It thrills me to find here and there among the foolishness of science fiction miracles that remind me of the miracles of the Bible and make me think, "Some day we will understand how such things can be."

Among the Old Testament myths, as some would call them, is the story of a healing, and more than a healing, which goes from step to step to show the growth of faith and power in a woman by the work of the prophet Elisha. I have not tried to analyze, study, prove or disprove, stories of axheads or cruses of oil or flying chariots. My searchlight does not reach that far. I simply leave them on the table, as it were, saying, "Some day we will learn enough of the laws of life to enable us to understand these things." But the story of the Shunammite woman I can come near to understanding, since it is a chronicle of faith and healing. So I will comment upon it in some detail.

The story begins with a woman of Shunam taking note of the prophet Elisha.

"And she said unto her husband, Behold now, I perceive that this is an holy man of God, which passeth by us continually. Let us make a little chamber, I pray thee, on the wall; and let us set for him there a bed, and a table, and a stool, and a candlestick: and it shall be, when he cometh to us, that he shall turn in thither. And it fell on a day, that he came thither, and he turned into the chamber, and lay there." (2 Kings 4:9-11)

I can see in my mind the little chamber on the wall. I imagine stone steps going up the outside of the flat house, and on top of the wall a sort of penthouse elegantly furnished with a bed and a table and a stool and a candlestick. Who could desire more?

Elisha said to his servant, "Call this Shunammite. And when he had called her, she stood before him. And he said unto him, Say now unto her, Behold, thou hast been careful for us with all this care; what is to be done for thee?" (2 Kings 4:12-13)

It seems strange, perhaps, that Elisha should not speak directly to the woman at this point. Instead, he asked his servant to call her. But, having been born and brought up in China, I can understand this. It is a mark of dignity and respect that a visiting gentleman should not speak directly to a woman. In fact, in China a married woman was not called by any particular name of her own. My cook used to lean out of the window and say, "Ta hai-tse ti niang!" ("Mother of those children") by which term he hailed his wife.

So Elisha asked the woman through his servant, "Wouldest thou be spoken for to the king, or to the captain of the host? And she answered, I dwell among mine own people," and apparently she turned and went away. Elisha said to the servant, "What then is to be done for her? And Gehazi answered, Verily she hath no child, and her husband is old. And he said, Call her. And when he had called her, she stood in the door. And he said, About this season, according to the time of life, thou shalt embrace a son." (2 Kings 4:13-16)

The prophet simply seized upon the spiritual power with which God had endowed him. I trust that before doing so he lifted up his heart unto the Lord, asked for guidance, and heard the Lord say, "Yes." At any rate he connected himself with a current of God's energy and projected it by an act of faith into the body of the woman. And as he did this he stated aloud the word of faith, even as Jesus did. "Young man, I say unto thee, Arise," Jesus said. (Luke 7:14) "Thy son liveth," Jesus said. (John 4:50) "Rise, take up thy bed, and walk," Jesus said. (John 5:8) So said Elisha, "Thou shalt embrace a son."

Every miracle in the Old Testament and in the New Testament took place through someone's direct, absolute flatfooted expression of complete faith. If Elisha had said, "Oh Lord, please let this good, deserving woman have a child if it be Thy will," presumably she would not have been healed of her barrenness. Instead he said, "This shall be so." And as I have pointed out in all my books, this is the meaning of "Amen." And it is this word of faith that is the word of power that sets God's creative light in motion. Note however that in the beginning the woman herself had no faith. It was her goodness to the prophet which moved him to a deed of gratitude, and her lack of faith did not stand in the way of his word of power.

The woman herself indeed answered, rather amusingly, "Nay, my Lord, thou man of God, do not lie unto thine handmaid." (2 Kings 4:16) Neverthless she "conceived, and bare a son at that season that Elisha had said unto her, according to the time of life." And when the child was grown, it fell on a day, that he went out to his father to the reapers. And he said unto his father, "My head, my head." (We might say today that the child suffered sunstroke, or possibly was suddenly taken with meningitis.) His father said to a lad, "Carry him to his mother. And when he had taken him, and brought him to his mother, he sat on her knees till noon, and then died." (2 Kings 4:19-20)

We can imagine the picture. We may be sure that as he sat on her knees this woman prayed. We know it because the rest of the story shows us how tremendously her faith had grown though *seeing* a miracle, even as the faith of those who followed Jesus grew because they *saw* His works. Some people say we should believe without even seeing any miracles, but Jesus did not say that. He said, on the other hand, that the same power that was in Him could be in us. (Luke 24:49) He stated that we should do the works that He did. (John 14:12) He told us that we should go into all the world, and not only preach the gospel to every creature, but show forth the power of the gospel by healing. (Mark 16:15-18)

As we see miracles, faith comes to us as it came to the Shunammite woman. There was nothing else that she could do except to pray. There were no doctors; there were no telephones; there was nothing except God.

Nevertheless, in spite of all her prayer, the child died.

What did she do then? Did she say, "I must accept the will of God"? No, she did not, because she knew that this was not the will of God. She did not commit the sin that so many people commit, believing that every terrible thing that happens is of necessity the will of God. Whether she understood the work of the enemy I do not know, but this I do know: she believed that it was God's will for her child to live.

"And she went up, and laid him on the bed of the man of God, and shut the door upon him, and went out." (2 Kings 4:21) Why did she take him there? Why did she not put him upon his own bed? I am sure she had a feeling that the presence of God, the actual radiation of the power of God, was more strong and more real in the room where the prophet had slept than it would have been in any other room.

A church wherein many prayers have been said is filled with the power of God. A sensitive person can feel it as soon as he enters the door. Every church should be filled with the power of God. A church should be a place where miracles happen. How tragic that in many churches the power is so cold, so faint and dim, that one cannot feel it! And yet how comforting that there are churches today in which the power of God is as real as a light, or a sort of radiation, so that people say, "It feels like electricity in the air!"

The woman left the body of her son in Elisha's room and went down to the field. "And she called unto her husband, and said, Send me, I pray thee, one of the young men, and one of the asses, that I may run to the man of God, and come again. And he said, Wherefore wilt thou go to him today? it is neither new moon, nor sabbath. And she said, It shall be well." (2 Kings 4:22-23)

She was holding to her faith with all the power and strength that she had. She did not wish to weaken this even by saying aloud that the lad was dead. So she said, the words of her mouth carrying out the belief of her heart, "It shall be well."

"Then she saddled an ass, and said to her servant, Drive, and go forward; slack not thy riding for me, except I bid thee." (2 Kings 4:24)

Perhaps you who read cannot quite picture this scene. I can; I have ridden a little donkey across he plains with a lad running behind hitting him from time to time in order to speed his progress. It is not a comfortable means of travel!

How perfectly amazing! I wonder whether Elisha had instructed her concerning the power of the spoken word or whether she just simply knew it, having seen it working in her own life. But she did know it. Even though her son was dead she would not say those words aloud lest they fasten death upon him, but said with her lips that which she desired with her heart, "It shall be well."

This is one of the principles of the prayer of faith. Not only should we utter our prayer in most positive words, saying in conclusion, "It shall be so," or, "Thank you Lord, your will shall be done, and your power shall prevail, and this person shall be well." But also we should watch our lips from that time forth, and should refrain from moaning and complaining and saying words of fear about the subject of our prayer.

Now could I dare to believe that my son would be raised from the dead? I am not sure. In fact I doubt it very much. And yet we do sometimes work for a resurrection, as in cases of drowning, and in cases where a person's heart stops during an operation, when doctors use every means of resuscitation that they know, feeling rightly that the spirit of the person is not very far away. Moreover, I have heard of prayers for the healing even of the dead, and in the end of this chapter I will tell of an incident of this kind wherein my prayers may have helped to bring life to "the miracle baby" (to quote the words of doctors and nurses).

But to return to the woman of Shunam: she said nothing except that word of faith, "It shall be well," but she acted immediately and with vigor.

"So she went and came unto the man of God to mount Carmel. And it came to pass, when the man of God saw her afar off, that he said to Gehazi his servant, Behold, yonder is that Shunammite: run now, I pray thee, to meet her, and say unto her, Is it well with thee? is it well with thy husband? is it well with the child? And she answered, It is well." (2 Kings 4:25-26) She was looking into the future and seeing in her mind the little boy well, and she was saying with her lips the thing that she believed would be.

"And when she came to the man of God to the hill, she caught him by the feet." There again I can see the picture: the woman in her anguish falling on the ground before him and reaching out her hands unto his feet. "But Gehazi came near to thrust her away. And the man of God said, Let her alone; for her soul is vexed within her: and the Lord hath hid it from me, and hath not told me." (2 Kings 4:27) Apparently he was surprised at this, for those who pray together are close in spirit, and frequently are aware of troubles even from a distance.

"Then she said, Did I desire a son of my lord? did I

not say, Do not deceive me?" She was still unwilling to put into words the fact that the son was dead. She made a statement therefore by asking a question, in thoroughly Oriental fashion. "Then he said to Gehazi, Gird up thy loins, and take my staff in thine hand, and go thy way: if thou meet any man, salute him not; and if any salute thee, answer him not: and lay my staff upon the face of the child." (2 Kings 4:28-29)

The servant was no doubt younger and stronger than Elisha, and could travel more rapidly. Elisha simply told him to wrap his trailing robes around him, so as to get them out of the way—in other words, to prepare to run, as a runner would do today by putting on shorts —and to take his master's staff and lay it upon the face of the child. Is it possible that an object, a staff, could convey a sense of spiritual presence or spiritual power? Certainly it would seem to be possible! Many people use a cross or a holy medal in this very same way today.

We can see that a living person can be comforted by such a sign. But how could the child, being dead, perceive it? Here we come upon great mysteries. The body of the child was lifeless. But where was the spirit of the child? Not too far away, I imagine, not too far away. And the spirit of the child surely could perceive in the rod the presence and the power of the prophet. The rod that Elisha usually held in his hand could actually, as a matter of fact, be saturated with the radiation of spiritual power that was in Elisha. There was once a woman who touched the hem of Jesus' garment, and power flowed from Him through that cloth. (Matt. 9:20-22) I could tell a marvelous story of a girl who lay at the door of death and when her lips touched the spoon in which were the sacred elements, the body and blood of Christ administered by the priest, apparently her spirit sensed and felt the power, and she returned to life.

"And the mother of the child said, As the Lord liveth, and as thy soul liveth, I will not leave thee. And he arose and followed her. And Gehazi passed on before them, and laid the staff upon the face of the child; but there was neither voice, nor hearing. Wherefore he went again to meet him, and told him, saying, The child is not awakened. And when Elisha was come into the house, behold, the child was dead, and laid upon his bed." (2 Kings 4:30-32) The prophet checked on the child, and yes, the body was cold and still. Elisha was not a young man. He knew death when he saw it; the child was dead.

"He went in therefore, and shut the door upon them twain, and prayed unto the Lord. And he went up, and lay upon the child, and put his mouth upon his mouth, and his eyes upon his eyes, and his hands upon his hands: and he stretched himself upon the child; and the flesh of the child waxed warm." (2 Kings 4:33-34) In healing today, in passing on the blessing of God through all the long history of the church, the laying-on of hands has been used: the contact of one body with another body, so that even the body may be a channel of the living power of God. In this case, the child being dead, apparently the prophet sensed that the laying on of hands was not sufficient. He stretched himself upon the child. He moved so as to touch the child's eyes, the child's hands, the child's mouth, with those parts of his own body. He breathed into his mouth the breath of life, even as a person does today for one recently drowned.

As Elisha so lent his own body to be a channel of the living power of God, the flesh of the child waxed warm. But Elisha did not stay there and continue praying. "Then he returned, and walked in the house to and fro." (2 Kings 4:35) Prayer is work. It demands a tremendous amount of spiritual energy. Elisha felt his body becoming stretched and strained with weariness. Therefore he ceased praying for a while, and walked to and fro in the house. Just as there is power in praying, there is also power in ceasing to pray. In the old days when I prayed for the sick with tremendous insistence, I found that if I ceased praying for a while and walked to and fro in the house, probably making beds and picking up children's clothes and putting them in the closet, then I could return to my prayer with increased energy.

So Elisha returned, "And went up, and stretched himself upon him: and the child sneezed seven times, and the child opened his eyes." (2 Kings 4:35) I said to a doctor once, "I don't understand about the sneezing; that seems so silly."

The doctor said, "Not at all; that was clearing out the mucus from the passages of breathing."

The child opened his eyes. And Elisha called Gehazi, and said, "Call this Shunammite. So he called her. And when she was come in unto him, he said, Take up thy son. Then she went in, and fell at his feet, and bowed herself to the ground, and took up her son, and went out." (2 Kings 4:36-37)

Have I ever known such a thing as this to happen today? In a smaller way, yes. There was a young woman giving birth to a baby during the war, and the family had not been able to find a doctor. She had had convulsions for twenty-four hours. When a doctor finally came to her, he said, "The baby is gone; there is no hope for the baby, but we will try to save the mother." The mother of the woman in childbirth called me and asked for prayers. I prayed and simply imagined the light of God surrounding mother and child, bringing forth life in whatever way was best. The doctor delivered the baby a half hour later under heavy opiates, the mother's convulsions, of course, having stopped immediately. The baby was dead; it was blue and cold. They made no effort to bring it to life. Humanly speaking, this was impossible. They laid it aside, not even covering it. Two hours later the young mother awoke and wanted to see the baby. The nurse told her, "The baby is dead."

She said, "Bring me the baby. I want to baptize it, alive or dead."

In telling me the story later on she said, "I regret one thing: I was so confused that I couldn't think of any other name but my own, and I don't think it's a very pretty name. But I put some water on her head, and I said, "I baptize you Caroline, in the name of the Father, and of the Son, and of the Holy Ghost."

And the baby's flesh waxed warm; and the baby opened her eyes; and the baby lived!

8
Job

✳

We are told in the prologue to this three-act play that God held a sort of party, or corroboree, up in the heavens, and all the sons of God gathered together. These great and mysterious beings are mentioned now and again in the Bible. "When the morning stars sang together, and all the sons of God shouted for joy." (Job 38:7) Who are they?

Some of them will appear later in time, as we reckon time, in the book of Job. Some of them, through the power and operation of the Holy Spirit, will emerge in and through living people upon the earth, and for this, as St. Paul points out, the whole creation abides, waiting for the manifestation of the sons of God. (Rom. 8:19)

But although we do not like to face the fact, God is not limited to this planet earth. We are used to thinking of ourselves as the center of the created universe. Unfortunately (or fortunately) astronomers are shattering this comfortable illusion. How many other universes God may have, how many other suns, how many living creatures of different ranks and orders, we do not know. But before the earth was born, there were the sons of God, and they gathered together to worship and adore Him.

Then we are told that Satan also came among them. (Job 1:6) Certain psychologists delight in mentioning Satan as one of the sons of God. Let me point out that Satan is nowhere thus described in the Bible. Rather, he crashed the party, as it were. The word "also" denotes that he was an outsider, not an invited guest. The sons of God seem to have been of a higher order even than the angels.

Satan though not a son of God was a creation of God. So are you: so am I. So is the worst criminal lurking in a cell, or dangerously roaming the countryside, looking for God's little ones, that he may violate them. A sexual maniac was made with the potentiality of becoming at least a child of God, but he has not become one. Satan was probably created with the potentiality of becoming one of the high and holy ones, but he did not fulfill that potentiality. Nevertheless in some way Satan had access to the heavens. "And Satan also came among them." (Job 1:6)

I am a dramatist, having written plays, directed plays, acted in them, done make-up, and designed stage-settings. I know a play when I see one. Therefore, as I read the book of Job, I perceive that this is a poetic three-act drama, with a prologue and an epilogue of prose. The prologue gives the fascinating picture of God entertaining the sons of God in the heavens, and among them, Satan. No doubt, if this play was enacted long ago, a man would have taken the part of God and another man the part of Satan. We can envision these parts being acted in any way that our fancy might direct. Imagine it thus as you read this introduction, and see how it comes to life!

"And the Lord said unto Satan, Whence comest thou? Then Satan answered the Lord, and said, From going to and fro in the earth, and from walking up and down in it. And the Lord said unto Satan, Hast thou considered my servant Job, that there is none like him in the earth, a perfect and an upright man, one that feareth God, and escheweth evil? Then Satan answered the Lord, and said, Doth Job fear God for nought? . . . Thou hast blessed the work of his hands, and his substance is increased in the land. But put forth thine hand now, and touch all that he hath, and he will curse thee to thy face. And the Lord said unto Satan, Behold, all that he hath is in thy power; only upon himself put not

forth thine hand. So Satan went forth from the presence
of the Lord." (Job 1:7-12)

What truth can there be in this ancient presentation
of the power of good and the power of evil? Great
truth, it seems to me, and I have seen it more than once
in my own little walk upon this earth. A man who is
good and righteous in all his ways is a challenge to the
enemy, the power of evil. He is therefore in more danger
from Satan than is anyone else, unless he be surrounded
by the protection of Christ. Christ had not yet come
upon the earth to pour forth His life as a bulwark
against the power of evil. Therefore, in a sense, all
that Job had was open to the destructive power of
Satan. Yet the power of God remained greater than
Satan's power, and the person of Job himself could
not be destroyed by the enemy.

Why then was Job in the hands of the enemy and
under the power of Satan? Was that God's will and intention? Surely not. Remember our first chapters. God
made man and put him upon this earth, and made available to him powers both of good and of evil, and gave
man the ability to choose between them. The old question raises it head again and again—why did God do so?
Why did God not automatically so create the universe
that there was no possibility of evil?

We have meditated upon this in earlier chapters, and
yet our meditations have all come to the one answer
that there is no answer—namely, we do not know. But
such is the plan of the universe. The universe itself
swings upon the stresses and strains of a balance between darkness and light. Men also must balance continually between good and evil. If man had chosen only
good from the beginning, if Cain had not slain his
brother Abel, if destruction had never been let loose
upon this earth, then surely Satan would not have been
able to touch the flocks and herds and sons and daughters of Job. But the power of destruction had been let
loose upon this earth. The thought-forms of destruction
filled the air; the currents of destructive energy and
power were present in the air, invisible but real. There-

fore, when God said to Satan, "Behold, he is in thine hand," God was merely stating a fact.

The destruction of Satan came upon the flocks and herds and sons and daughters of Job until nothing was left. Satan had said to God that if this should happen, Job would curse God to His face. (Job 1:11) Job rent his mantle and shaved his head, and fell down upon the ground, but he did not curse God. He worshiped God, and said, "Naked came I out of my mother's womb, and naked shall I return thither: the Lord gave, and the Lord hath taken away; blessed be the name of the Lord." (Job 1:21)

This foundation of trust without any understanding, of faith that exists no matter what happens, is the foundation upon which all our prayers for healing should be laid. True, we can create in our minds the picture of the person well. True, we can send forth the prayer of faith, and we can hope that the power of prayer will return into us, bringing healing. But sometimes healing does not come, and we may not understand the reasons any more than Job understood the reasons. Great are we then in the Lord's sight when with Job we can say, "The Lord gave, and the Lord hath taken away; blessed be the name of the Lord." Or indeed as Job said later in this same wonderful book: "Though He slay me, yet will I trust in Him." (Job 13:15)

Now we, looking back through time, can achieve a glimmer of understanding. At least we know what Job was fighting: that combined and massed power of evil that seeks to destroy a man who is righteous. He was fighting the enemy, Satan. As St. Paul said long afterward, "We wrestle not against flesh and blood, but against principalities, against powers, against the rulers of the darkness of this world, against spiritual wickedness in high places." (Eph. 6:12) In the very beginning of the Bible we read of the coming of the enemy upon this earth. But somehow in the dark ages it was forgotten, even as today it is widely forgotten. Many people say, "Why did God do this?" when God did not do it at all; it was Satan who did it. It is stylish nowadays for people to believe that there really is no enemy, that there is not actually any satanic power, that this is only imagination, or a symbolic or fanciful way of saying something. And as we held this concept, we too are likely to fall into the trap that the enemy lays for us, and to endure the persecution of this enemy who, no matter what we think, is real and terrible and full of dark power.

Job did not understand this. Nevertheless he retained his integrity. He did not curse God. Again there was another day when the sons of God came to present themselves before the Lord, and Satan also came among them. And again there was a conversation between the two. "And the Lord said unto Satan, Hast thou considered my servant Job, that there is none like him in the earth, a perfect and an upright man, one that feareth God, and escheweth evil? and still he holdeth fast his integrity, although thou movedst me against him, to destroy him without cause. And Satan answered the Lord, and said, Skin for skin, yea, all that a man hath will he give for his life. But put forth thine hand now, and touch his bone and his flesh, and he will curse thee to thy face. And the Lord said unto Satan, Behold, he is in thine hand; but save his life. So went Satan forth from the presence of the Lord, and smote Job with sore boils from the sole of his foot unto his crown. . . . Then said his wife unto him, Dost thou still retain thine integrity? curse God, and die. But he said unto her, Thou speakest as one of the foolish women speaketh. What? Shall we receive good at the hand of God, and shall we not receive evil? In all this did not Job sin with his lips." (Job 2:3-10)

"Put forth thine hand," said the enemy to God. But God said to the enemy, "He is in *thine* hand!"—the old struggle, the never-ending swing between good and evil. Now Job did not know that while in the first place all came from God, in the second place man's choice of evil had given power to the enemy. He believed that all of his trouble came purposely and willfully from

God. Nevertheless, he accepted it with humility and did not sin with his lips. What a man!

If Job had lived after Jesus Christ came into the world, it need not have been thus. Job sensed trouble coming: he knew fear. "For the thing which *I greatly feared* is come upon me, and that which I was afraid of is come unto me." (Job 3:25) So he said. He could have talked to God and said, "What is this, Lord? I feel a premonition; I feel fear." And the Lord could have said to him, "There is danger from the enemy. Surround yourself with protection. Call upon the light of Jesus Christ to be around you, and this power from the enemy will come up against that surrounding force, and will turn back and go away, for it will not be able to get through."

But in these old days (for we are told by some that the book of Job is the oldest in the Bible) Jesus had not yet come. Nevertheless, Job, though not understanding, retained his faith in God.

However, he had not the slightest intention of retaining his illness. We speak of "the patience of Job," but it does not seem to me that patience is quite the correct word for this man. He had an unshakable faith, that is true, but patience he did not have! He screamed, he yelled, he protested, he defended himself against God and against the three friends who came to console him. He had no feeling whatsoever that by being sick he glorified God.

Yes, three friends came to console him, and as we read their consolations, we do not know whether to laugh or cry, because every single one of them told Job that his trouble came upon him by his own fault. They said in effect, as people sometimes say today, "If you had had more faith, this would not have happened." Or, "You must be living in sin." Or, "Search yourself; try and know yourself, and see what dark thing in you has brought this upon you." Thus they spake, and Job said unto them, "Miserable comforters are ye all." (Job 16:2)

Job could not be talked down. He defended himself

against their charges, and he had a right to defend himself. In the first place, their charges were not true, for we are told specifically that Job was a righteous man, and even the devil saw that and admitted it. In the second place, even if they had been true, it would have been no consolation and no kindness for his friends to come and tell him so.

There are "Job's comforters" today. When we fail in a prayer for healing it is a human temptation to go to the person and say, "Now what is the block? Look into yourself and see what barriers are in your life," or to say, "If only you had had enough faith, you would have been healed." This is not kind, and very likely it is not true. Certainly some evils that befall a person are the result of his own sin, his own lack of harmony, his own lack of forgiveness. But other evils that befall a righteous person are specifically and exactly the result of the temptations of the enemy and the attacks of the enemy upon him. They may come from such a deep inner sorrow that possibly one does not really want to live. And whence comes this deep inner sorrow but from the enemy?

"Yea, . . . ye dig a pit for your friend," so said Job. (Job 6:27) And later he remarked, still arguing with his three friends: "Are not my days few? cease then, and let me alone, that I may take comfort a little, before I go whence I shall not return, even to the land of darkness and the shadow of death; a land of darkness, as darkness itself; and of the shadow of death, without any order, and where the light is as darkness." (Job 10:20-22)

Jesus had not come, and Job did not know that beyond the land of darkness and the shadow of death there is a land that Jesus called paradise. (Luke 23:43) And beyond that there is the high glory of heaven, and of the heaven of heavens, and the brightness of eternity that goes on forever in a light so brilliant that it cannot be seen by the human eye. Job did not know this. The Bible is a wonderful collection of manuscripts showing forth true and glorious things about God and man. But these revelations came to man step by step, and so they are recounted. So Job sat upon the dung heap and scraped himself with a potsherd (Job 2:8) while his wife from time to time urged him to forget the whole thing, to curse God and die. And his three friends sat upon the ground round about him and poured out sententious words, mouthing rounded sentences concerning the goodness of God, and the iniquity of Job, the secret sins that he had within his soul.

On and on it went. An American audience would never have sat through this play, but I know that an Oriental audience would have done so, going out perhaps to get a cup of tea and some peanuts, and coming back to continue their enjoyment. And I have no doubt that in the ancient days of Job, if this really were enacted as a play (which I imagine it was) it would not have seemed long and tedious.

Nobody, however, could talk Job down, and in Chapter 12, verses 2-3, he says, "No doubt but ye are the people, and wisdom shall die with you. But I have understanding as well as you; I am not inferior to you." And again (Job 13:1-5), "Lo, mine eye hath seen all this, mine ear hath heard and understood it. What ye know, the same do I know also: I am not inferior unto you. Surely I would speak to the Almighty, and I desire to reason with God. But ye are forgers of lies, ye are all physicians of no value. O that ye would altogether hold your peace! and it should be your wisdom."

Again Job answered and said, "How long will ye vex my soul, and break me in pieces with words? These ten times have ye reproached me: ye are not ashamed that ye make yourselves strange to me. And be it indeed that I have erred, mine error remaineth with myself." (Job 19:2-4) Or as we might say, "Suppose I have done wrong; that's my business and not yours."

"For I know that my redeemer liveth," said Job, "and that he shall stand at the latter day upon the earth: and though after my skin worms destroy this body, yet in my flesh shall I see God: whom I shall see for myself, and mine eyes shall behold, and not another; though my reins be consumed within me." (Job 19:25-27)

Now what in the world did he mean? He has already said that he believes that he shall go down into the grave, and that there is no light in that land of darkness. Did he look far through the future, and did he glimpse with the eyes of the spirit, even though his conscious mind did not understand it, his redeemer, the Lord Jesus Christ, standing upon this earth? Did he know that even though his "skin" should die, there was another body, a spiritual body, that someday in a miraculous manner would become a resurrection body, like the body of Jesus Himself—a body that could appear in the flesh, or could disappear, a body that retained all the soundness and all the humanity of life upon this earth, and that nevertheless was eternal in the heavens? How could he know this?

How do all of us from time to time know things that the conscious mind cannot grasp? how is it that with all of us, or at least with many of us, from time to time the clouds part, and we have a little glimpse of the sunlight beyond? And even though at the moment we may not be able to reconcile it to the darkness that surrounds us, nevertheless we have seen it and we know it.

Job is known as a holy man not because he was stricken with boils and bereaved of his children, his flocks, and his herds, but because he would not surrender to these misfortunes. He would not curse God and die; he would not be merely passively patient, but he sought and strove after God with everything that was in him. So the spirit of Job leaped far ahead of his mind, and he saw things that he could not possibly understand. Therefore he said words that to this day are sung in every church, words of beauty and glory that live forever. "Oh that my words were now written! oh that they were printed in a book," he said, "that they were graven with an iron pen and lead in the rock for ever!" (Job 19:23-24) They are not only printed in a book but they are graven upon the hearts of all Christians. They are indeed embedded in the rock of the church of Jesus Christ forever.

In spite of these inspired words, however, the mind of Job continued to seek, and continued to wonder, continued to question with unanswerable questions. "Wherefore do the wicked live," he asked, "become old, yea, are mighty in power?" (Job 21:7) He was not the first one to ask this question, nor is he the last. Jesus gave us the answer, saying that the wheat and the tares will be rooted up, and only the wheat will remain. (Matt. 13:24-30).

But all of this was far ahead, and Job could not see it. In Chapter 23 he says, "Oh that I knew where I might find him! that I might come even to his seat! I would order my cause before him, and fill my mouth with arguments. I would know the words which he would answer me and understand what he would say unto me. Will he plead against me with his great power? No; but he would put strength in me. . . . Behold, I go forward, but he is not there; and backward, but I cannot perceive him: on the left hand, where he doth work, but I cannot behold him: he hideth himself on the right hand, that I cannot see him." (Job 23:3-6,8-9)

The tenor of Job's complaint has changed. He began by seeking, and indeed demanding to know the reason for this persecution which he thought was a persecution by God. He complained in loud and anguished tones about the nature of his illnesses and troubles. But now his complaint is that he cannot find God! Now the desire of his heart is to see God, to know God. Now he is seeking not so much for understanding, not so much for justification nor for healing, as he is seeking to know God himself.

This change takes place in many people. In my own experience, I began to endeavor to understand the laws of God in order to pray for healing for myself and for others. But now I am more interested just in knowing God. As one goes on seeking God for healing, one's spirit more and more becomes open to Him, so that the time does come when one seeks God for Himself.

There are people who demand of those who are sick and in trouble that they begin with "giving themselves to God." My dear friends, this does not work! When people are sick and in mental depression it is no good to say to them, "But it doesn't matter about getting well; you should seek God first of all." They cannot; they are too sick; they are too miserable. They need first to seek for healing. But as they learn how to pray, as in any way whatsoever they enter into the presence of God, then after a while as the light of God begins to dawn upon them, they care more about God than they care about anything that God can do. So we lead them gently into the presence of God.

The friends of Job did not lead him gently. Nevertheless, by the maintaining of his own faith in spite of everything, he came to a place where the desire of his heart was to see God Himself.

When Job began to desire to see God Himself, then the way opened more and more that he *should* see God. "As God liveth, who hath taken away my judgment," says Job, "and the Almighty, who hath vexed my soul; all the while my breath is in me, and the spirit of God is in my nostrils; my lips shall not speak wickedness, nor my tongue utter deceit." (Job 27:2-4) And in Chapter 31:38-40: "If my land cry against me, or that the furrows likewise thereof complain; if I have eaten the fruits thereof without money, or have caused the owners thereof to lose their life: let thistles grow instead of wheat, and cockle instead of barley. The words of Job are ended."

To the very end Job maintained his innocence, and Job was right. Take note of this final declaration. What was the greatest sin of which Job could conceive? It was a sin against the land. It was a sin of dishonesty, or misuse of the gifts of God provided in the fruits of the land, and in the money that should come from the fruits of the land.

With this final cry the words of Job were ended. Then there arose a young man whose anger was kindled against him. He did not believe that the reproaches of

Job's three friends were kind or wise, and he spoke forth, adding his opinion to theirs. "Behold, in this thou art not just," says Elihu. "I will answer thee, that God is greater than man. Why dost thou strive against him? for he giveth not account of any of his matters. For God speaketh once, yea twice, yet man perceiveth it not. In a dream, in a vision of the night, when deep sleep falleth upon men, in slumberings upon the bed; then he openeth the ears of men, and sealeth their instruction." (Job 33:12-16)

Elihu here is saying two things: first, that God does not choose to explain to man all of His reasons, that man's salvation does not depend entirely upon understanding either God or himself. Second, that although God does tell man as much as He can, as much as man is able to grasp, still man does not sufficiently heed it or carry it out. It is fascinating that Elihu mentions here the fact that God communicates to man in dreams, in a deep sleep upon his bed at night. Psychology nowadays is taking notice of this fact, but actually it is not a new concept. In the story of Joseph, found in the latter part of Genesis, a great deal is said about this fact: that God can communicate with the deep subconscious mind of man in sleep even when the conscious mind is not able to hear Him. This is not God's only way of speaking to man. Those who seek God in high contemplation can sometimes hear Him when they are awake. When a man can speak with his friend directly, face to face, he does not need to take so much time to write letters and to read his friend's letters. Often, however, God takes a time when the conscious mind is not functioning, and presents things to the unconscious mind in dreams. The unconscious mind is not always able to communicate with us in direct words but uses symbols to convey ideas.

Psychology helps us to learn some of these symbols, to increase our awareness of what the unconscious mind is trying to say. I have learned much about this from my son's book, *Dreams: God's Forgotten Language*. But how wonderful that long before anyone ever thought of psychology, Elihu said to Job that God communicated with him in dreams! Elihu did not try to teach Job to understand his dreams; but he continued to speak in a way that released Job from his bondage. He went far beyond Job's problems. He did not try to explain why illness and trouble came upon him, but spoke in quaint old words to Job of the glory of God, reading God in the world that God has made. "Behold, God is great," he says, "and we know him not, neither can the number of his years be searched out. For he maketh small the drops of water: they pour down rain according to the vapour thereof: which the clouds do drop and distil upon man abundantly. Also can any understand the spreadings of the clouds, or the noise of his tabernacle? Behold, he spreadeth his light upon it, and covereth the bottom of the sea. For by them judgeth he the people; he giveth meat in abundance. With clouds he covereth the light; and commandeth it not to shine by the cloud that cometh betwixt. The noise thereof sheweth concerning it, the cattle also concerning the vapour." (Job 36:26-33)

"Hearken unto this, O Job," Elihu says in the next chapter, "stand still, and consider the wondrous works of God. Dost thou know when God disposed them, and caused the light of his cloud to shine? Dost thou know the balancings of the clouds, the wondrous works of him which is perfect in knowledge?" (Job 37:14-16) So Elihu directed the thinking of Job away from his troubles, away from his perplexities and his self-searching, and directly into the glory of God. As Job forgot himself, and as his soul arose to a contemplation of the wonder of God, he heard the voice of God. He perceived the glory of God. He had a cosmic experience. The doors of his spirit opened, showed him things that are invisible, and gave him a feeling of the greatness of God that cannot be expressed in words. The book endeavors to express it, and the words are beautiful, and yet I know that no words can fully express it.

I remember when some such experience first happened to me. There is no explaining it; there is no recapturing of it; there is no expressing of it. For a split second I lived in the glory of heaven, and the bliss of it was so great that I thought, "If this does not stop, I will surely die." And then I thought, "But I do not want it to stop!"

Job in the book makes no attempt to explain how he felt, and Job is wise, for words cannot convey even the first beginning of the dawning of that light. Job therefore speaks only of that which man can see: of God's creation; and he speaks of it in the words of God Himself. "Then the Lord answered Job out of the whirlwind, and said, Who is this that darkeneth counsel by words without knowledge? Gird up now thy loins like a man; for I will demand of thee, and answer thou me. Where wast thou when I laid the foundations of the earth? declare, if thou hast understanding. Who hast laid the measures thereof, if thou knowest? or who hath stretched the line upon it? Whereupon are the foundations thereof fastened? or who laid the corner stone thereof; when the morning stars sang together, and all the sons of God shouted for joy?" (Job 38:1-7)

This is a picture beyond the farthest grasp of our understanding. Those who seek for knowledge in the world of science show us more and more alarming and glorious and utterly shattering truths concerning this universe and its creation. Can we imagine ourselves standing there at the beginning of it, when all the sons of God shouted for joy? No, we cannot. Neither, I am sure, could Job, and yet something in him sensed it. Something in him entered into that glory, as the voice of the Lord came to him not relayed by anybody else, but directly, not shrouded in dreams but in the clear light of day.

"Out of whose womb came the ice?" said the voice of God, "And the hoary frost of heaven, who hath gendered it? The waters are hid as with a stone, and the face of the deep is frozen. Canst thou bind the sweet influence of the Pleiades, or loose the bands of Orion? Canst thou bring forth Mazzaroth in his season? or canst thou guide Arcturus with his sons? Knowest thou the ordinances of heaven? canst thou set the dominion thereof in the earth?" (Job 38:29-33)

Then God comes down from the sublime to the very common, and expounds to Job the fact that he could not create a horse. Moreover he points out to Job that leviathan, the whale, is beyond the power of Job to create or in any way to emulate. What is this? Surely Job knew that he could not create a horse, nor yet a whale. God did not have to come thundering out of heaven in order to inform Job of this very obvious fact, although—on second thought—do we always remember it? We are very proud of our creativity. We can make engines far more powerful than a horse. We can make engines that can devour the earth and plumb the sky and destroy hundreds of horses. And yet a thing that has life, that we cannot make. And if the time should come when with our infinite wisdom, or rather, with our finite wisdom, we destroy every living thing that is upon the earth—and such a time is not impossible—then what?

To return, however, to Job: What is the meaning of all this? The meaning of it is too great to be contained in words. The words are an attempt, I am sure, to explain what it was that Job really felt, for he entered into the creativity of God. He could feel in him a little bit of the power that goes forth to create horses and whales and all kinds of living creatures, and to command the rain and the raindrops and their treasures of the frost.

How do I know? For two reasons, and the first is that I have felt it. And second I know it by the results, for Job was healed. He experienced the flow of God's creative life within him, and he was healed. This I do not for one moment doubt, for I have known it to happen time and again. We strive after healing, and we are right to strive after healing. But the time comes when, striving after healing, we touch God, and our spirits communicate, and a door is really opened, and then the healing comes.

So Job says in the final chapter, "I have heard of thee by the hearing of the ear: but now mine eye seeth thee.

Wherefore I abhor myself, and repent in dust and ashes." (Job 42:5-6) Why did he repent? Of what did he repent? He had proclaimed his righteousness, and his righteousness was true. He did not sin against God in his heart, but maintained his faith through everything, and God honored and respected that faith. Of what then did Job repent? Only of the fact that until now he had never seen God. He had known Him with his conscious mind, but he had never seen Him. So in adoring God he abhorred himself, not in a destructive sense but in a sense of knowing the incomparable greatness of God as compared to the smallness of his little self.

To repent means to take a turn. It means to enter into a new life. When Job abhorred himself in his adoration of God, then the tide turned. First of all, the attitude of his three friends changed. They felt the command of God to apologize to Job, to offer sacrifices to him, to ask him to pray for them, to acknowledge him as a man far greater in spirit than they were or could ever be. And so they did. And furthermore, Job's body was apparently instantaneously made perfect, and all his friends returned to rejoice with him. "Then came there unto him all his brethren, and all his sisters, and all they that had been of his acquaintance before, and did eat bread with him in his house: and they bemoaned him, and comforted him over all the evil the Lord had brought upon him: every man also gave him a piece of money, and everyone an earring of gold. So the Lord blessed the latter end of Job more than his beginning." (Job 42:11-12)

And then we are told very quaintly the accounting of his sheep and camels and oxen and she-asses. Moreover, we are told that at his somewhat advanced age he proceeded to have seven sons and three daughters. And his daughters, amusingly and delightfully, apparently were really sensational! We are not told much about the sons; one hopes that they were fine young men, but the daughters were women beyond compare in their beauty and graciousness. "After this lived Job an hundred and forty years, and saw his sons, and his sons' sons, even four generations. So Job died, being old and full of days." (Job 42:16-17) And the glory of God was shown forth.

All of this I believe with my whole heart, and it rejoices me and uplifts my soul, and it delights and sometimes amuses my mind, for through the quaintness of this old imagery and these ancient words, there shines forth the glory of God.

9

Isaiah

✳

This, I do believe, is the most glorious book of the whole Old Testament. The sweep of Isaiah's poetry, the loftiness of his thinking, and the brilliance of his clear-cut logic are beyond compare. This book is enshrouded in music and is sung yearly during the festival seasons in Handel's *Messiah*. Surely one might think it needs no searchlight to illumine its meaning. And yet it most assuredly does, for part of its message has been totally ignored by Christians.

Many of course have searched its authorship, and with some reason. Critics say that Chapters 40-66 concern events that took place two hundred years later than the writing of the first Isaiah. They refer to its author as the Second Isaiah. However, this does not interest me, for the meaning of the book is not altered, whether the thoughts of two different men at different times were pooled together, or whether the same Isaiah looked two hundred years into the future.

Let me quote a summary of the opening chapters which is far more brilliant and concise than anything I could write:

> Isaiah's preface is in the form of a trial or assize. . . . It is a crown case, and God is at once plaintiff and judge. . . . The assessors are heaven and earth, whom the Lord's herald invokes to hear the Lord's plea. (v.2) The people of Judah are the defendants. The charge against them is one of brutish, ingrate stupidity breaking out into rebellion. The witness is the prophet himself. . . . The people's plea-in-defense,

laborious worship and multiplied sacrifice, is repelled and exposed. (v. 10-17) And the trial is concluded—Come now, let us bring our reasoning to a close, saith the Lord—by God's offer of pardon to a people thoroughly convicted. (v. 18)

God reasons with man—that is the first article of religion according to Isaiah. Revelation is not magical, but rational and moral. Religion is reasonable intercourse between one intelligent Being and another. . . .

Over against the prophetic view of religion sprawls and reeks in the same chapter the popular religion as smoky sacrifice, assiduous worship, and ritual. . . . [The people] . . . pray, they sacrifice, they solemnize to perfection. But they do not know, they do not consider . . . they do not *think*. "I cannot away," saith the Lord, "with wickedness and worship." (v. 13)

Would we be judged by our . . . temple-treading, which is Hebrew for church-going, by the wealth of our sacrifice, by our ecclesiastical position? This chapter (Isaiah 1) drags us out before the austerity and incorruptibleness of Nature. The assessors of the Lord are not the Temple nor the Law, but Heaven and Earth—not ecclesiastical conventions, but the grand moral fundamentals of the universe, purity, order and obedience to God.*

The book from which I have quoted is so magnificent that I would urge you to read it, both volumes. However, it was published in 1896! This does not alter its truth any more than the writing of the book of Isaiah hundreds of years before Christ alters its truth. But it may make it difficult for you to find it.

Now let us return to the Bible itself.

The victim of the people's sin is the land. "Your country is desolate, your cities are burned with fire: your land, strangers devour it in your presence and it is desolate." (Isa. 1:7)

We have not yet reached that stage, but those with eyes to see can behold its beginning. And those with the gift of prophecy tell us of the end that will be unless the

*George Adam Smith, *The Book of Isaiah* (1896), pp. 4-7.

people turn again unto the Lord so that He can save their land. (Isa. 55:6-13)

"Bring no more vain oblations. Incense is an abomination unto me," thundered Jahweh in the heart of the prophet. "The new moons and sabbaths, the calling of assemblies, I cannot away with; it is iniquity, even the solemn meeting. Your new moons and your appointed feasts my soul hateth: they are a trouble unto me; I am weary to bear them." (Isa. 1:13-14)

Why? Because, as he says in the next verses: "I will not hear: your hands are full of blood. Wash you, make you clean; put away the evil of your doings from before mine eyes; cease to do evil; learn to do well; seek judgment, relieve the oppressed, judge the fatherless, plead for the widow. . . . If ye be willing and obedient, ye shall eat the good of the land; but if ye refuse and rebel, ye shall be devoured with the sword: for the mouth of the Lord hath spoken it." (Isa. 1:15-20)

The Israelites went through all the forms of religion, even as we today go through all the forms of religion. Those forms were not unholy. In fact, the Spirit of God revealed to Moses these very ceremonies in which He would delight. The Holy Spirit decreed that there should be erected a place full of beauty and majesty that would suggest to people the lost holiness that was their birthright. But this had become unacceptable and altogether abominable to God because it was hypocrisy, because the very people who attended His assemblies and entered into His courts with thanksgiving were not keeping the laws. *Are we?*

We are also part of a nation. The sins of the nation are also our sins. The blood of our brothers in Vietnam is on our hands and shall be required of us. And no matter what we say about the honesty of our motives, the Lord God Almighty sees farther than our words. He knows the industries that grow fat on wars, and He knows the interests behind those industries that pull the strings that make the nations jump. There is nothing hidden that shall not some day be revealed (Matt. 10:26) and nothing wrong that must not some day be made right, for the mouth of the Lord hath spoken it.

"And it shall come to pass in the last days, that the mountain of the Lord's house [that is, the kingdom of the Lord] shall be established in the top of the mountains, and shall be exhalted above the hills: and all nations shall flow into it. And many people shall go and say, Come ye, and let us go up to the mountain of the Lord . . . and he will teach us of his ways, and we will walk in his paths. . . . And he shall judge among the nations, and shall rebuke many people: and they shall beat their swords into plowshares, and their spears into pruninghooks: nation shall not lift up sword against nation, neither shall they learn war any more." (Isa. 2:2-4)

The young man Isaiah was greatly troubled by these two conflicting types of pictures that came to him: the picture of the land laid waste and desolate, and the picture of the land, and indeed the nations, at peace. This latter picture, or concept, or prophecy even included disarmament and obviously a long and lasting peace. Very likely he wondered also why these contradictory bits of prophecy should have come to him. He no doubt prayed for guidance, saying, "Oh Lord, why are you showing me these things to come? What shall I do about them?"

So guidance came to him in a vision: a vision not of the future, either good or bad, but of the glory of God Himself. "I saw also the Lord sitting upon a throne, high and lifted up, and his train filled the temple." (Isa. 6:1)

Who were His train? Saints and angels, martyrs, and also strange living creatures that we know not, creatures not in the form of a man but in other forms, and to us totally incomprehensible. "Above it [the temple] stood the seraphims: each one had six wings; with twain he covered his face, and with twain he covered his feet, and with twain he did fly." (Isa. 6:2)

The seraphims: these are living beings who are not human, and have never lived upon the earth in a body of flesh. In times past only the most backward and most ignorant could believe in the existence of other living beings except those that we see in the flesh. Nowadays only the most backward and most ignorant of people can refuse to believe that there may be such living creatures in an unplumbed universe. Our most advanced scientists, and the most deep and wise among our intellectuals, are now searching for this very thing, having worked out by sheer intellect that the laws of life that created people upon this earth may have created God knows what kind of living beings upon other earths, probably not in this solar system but elsewhere in this unbelievably vast universe.

These living beings were mysteriously described as having six wings. With two they covered the face, so that the light and the glory of their faces should not shine forth upon this earth and scorch those who saw them. With two they covered their feet, so that their footsteps upon the psychic pathways of this world should not be heard. And with two they did fly, moving from here to there at the impulse of their wills, and at the impulse of God's will.

"And one cried unto another, and said, Holy, holy, holy, is the Lord of hosts: the whole earth is full of his glory. And the posts of the door moved at the voice of him that cried, and the house was filled with smoke." (Isa. 6:3-4) There are other references in the Bible to this filling of the house with a different kind of air, sometimes called smoke, sometimes called cloud. (E.g., Exod. 40:34; I Kings 8:10)

This is not hard for me to believe. During a mission as I sit in a front pew and wait for my time to speak, praying continually and fervently for the Holy Spirit to fill the church, I often see the chancel fill with something like a moving and shining mist. Sometimes even the posts or the walls of the chancel seem to shift within this mist, being not totally fixed in their places, but fluid, at it were. Sometimes different colors seem to run up and down them. I have seen this waking, with my eyes wide open, my spirit very alert, and my mind aware of everyone in the church. I am not in a trance in the sense of being separated from this earth, but I am keenly stimulated and aware both of this earth and of the invisible world in which we really live.

And so I can know what Isaiah saw when the temple seemed full of smoke, even the posts of the temple fluid and moving, no longer fixed in their places.

"Then said I, Woe is me! for I am undone; because I am a man of unclean lips, and I dwell in the midst of a people of unclean lips: for mine eyes have seen the King, the Lord of hosts." (Isa. 6:5) In the light and glory of the Lord, the shadows deepened upon this earth, even as when the sun arises in the morning, brilliantly lighting the mountaintops, the shadows are more strongly etched in the dark valleys between them.

"Then flew one of the seraphims unto me, having a live coal in his hand, which he had taken with the tongs from off the altar: and he laid it upon my mouth, and said, Lo, this hath touched thy lips; and thine iniquity is taken away, and thy sin purged." (Isa. 6:6-7) This Isaiah saw, whether literally or figuratively I do not know. But a light and a fire was taken from the altar. That fire was prepared by human hands, and the altar was built by human hands. The messenger of the Lord took what human beings had brought to Him with their own hands and their own wills, turned it into an agency of purity and forgiveness, and said unto Isaiah as it touched his lips that his sin was purged. He was set free from any bonds of the past.

He was set free to do what? No longer to look backward into himself. That was too trivial for a man set free by God Almighty! He was set free to look forward into the world; and the Lord immediately said, "Whom shall I send, and who will go for us? Then said I [Isaiah], Here am I: send me." (Isa. 6:8) He was set free to go and speak to the people of the holiness of God and of their need of repentance, of the terrible tribulations awaiting them if they did not repent, and also of the final promise of light and joy when they would finally turn to the Lord.

God knew, however, that what He told these people they would not at the moment understand or believe. Therefore, speaking in dramatic Oriental fashion, God said what sounds very strange to us. "Go, and tell this people, Hear ye indeed, but understand not; and see ye indeed, but perceive not. Make the heart of this people fat, and make their ears heavy, and shut their eyes; lest they see with their eyes, and hear with their ears, and understand with their heart, and convert, and be healed." (Isa. 6:9-10)

As we look back at this from the vantage point of our present day, we know that this is God's way of telling Isaiah to preach, even though many of the people would not hear and would not be converted. And those who heard and would not obey, would become more set in their own ways, rationalizing and persuading themselves that evil is good and that good is evil.

Isaiah spoke not merely to the individual but to the nation. In fact, all the prophets cry one theme—the healing of the land, the healing of the nation. We know now that the healing of the land and of the nation is through individuals and by individuals, but through the centuries of Judaism the priests and the Levites, the scribes and the Pharisees and the leaders tof the people, had to some extent lost sight of this. They tended to emphasize formal religious observances more than personal holiness. Therefore, as the Lord said most emphatically in the first chapter of Isaiah, the formal religious observances were no longer pleasing to Him but odious, and He would have nothing whatsoever to do with them.

Nevertheless, the final will of God is the salvation of the whole earth. (Isa. 66:1; Rev. 5:13) The Bible is so full of prophecies of the intermediate time of tribulation that we are apt to forget that the Creator will not be content until His little earth is saved. For this great purpose He has instructed us to pray, "Thy kingdom come. Thy will be done, in earth as it is in heaven." (Matt. 6:10)

A creator does not make something that it may be

destroyed. He creates it with the intention that it shall be good; it shall be perfect; it shall be beautiful. It is true that if He creates a thing that has a living will, such as a child born of father and mother, His purpose may not be fulfilled because of the rebellion of the child. There is the possibility that God's purpose upon this earth may not be fulfilled because of our rebellion, but there is also the absolute certainty that it is God's purpose to establish upon this earth the kingdom of heaven. "Then cometh the end, when he shall have delivered up the kingdom to God, even the Father; when he shall have put down all rule and all authority and power. For he must reign, till he hath put all enemies under his feet." (1 Cor. 15:24-25)

The kingdom of heaven is a "holy city," or a state of civilization wherein His will shall be done. It is His vineyard; it is His big business. This earth is His earth; this land is His land. The breath of His being is in every stick and stone, every tree and flower and mountain. Having once been incarnate upon the earth in the form of a living man, in one sense His being is forever incarnate upon and in this little earth whereon we walk. And He looks upon it with the same tender affection with which we look upon a garden that we tend, a farm that we till, trees that we plant. We love these spiritless objects—or are they quite spiritless?—with a deep and tender love. We probably inherit this love from our Father who created them. He loves this little earth with a deep and tender love; He broods upon it, He knows with anguish the tribulations that it will go through due to the foolishness of man, but nevertheless He loves it. And if we believe the words of the Scriptures, He will not give up, until it has become His kingdom. (Isa. 42:4)

Therefore, we also need to consider the healing of the earth, the healing especially of our own nation, even as Isaiah considered it. Isaiah shouted forth the sickness of his people because he knew that the land on which he lived needed to be forgiven and healed.

We in the United States for many years have blandly

assumed that we were in a sense the promised land: that ours was the best possible civilization, the best possible way of life. With great dismay we have begun to realize that this is not true, and that we also need the healing of our land in a very literal physical, as well as a spiritual, way. We have polluted our waters. We have polluted the air that we breathe with all kinds of radiation, fuel exhaust, and atomic fallout. Who knows how much of the increase of disease—cancer and leukemia, for instance—may be due to this poisoning of earth and air? In the very area where I live, men of business and science are soberly considering this fact. Some even say that within eight years we may have to prohibit automobiles run on gasoline. I do not know about this, but I do know that the earth itself is ill, is poisoned.

Our Lord spoke to the heart and to the soul of the individual. Nevertheless he did not lose sight of the goal, the kingdom of God. He compared the kingdom of God to a vineyard, to a farm, to a business. Take note of the fact that in none of His New Testament parables did the vineyard owner abandon the vineyard. He got rid of those servants who did not care for the vineyard in the right way and rebelled against Him, but the vineyard remained His. (E.g., Matt. 21:33-41) The big businessman did not give up his business; he dismissed the unfaithful steward, but he kept on with his business. (Luke 19:12-27)

Jesus also is keeping on with His business, and His business is, was, and shall be not only the healing and saving of the individual but also, in ways mysterious and far away, the healing and saving of the land. Jesus began with the individual. Isaiah began with the land, with the healing of the land, with the need of social reforms and repentance, and the re-establishment of righteousness in the land. For pages and pages therefore, from about Chapters 12 to 25, we hear the prophecies of doom upon the nations. This is frightening, and yet it is clothed in beauty. The book of Isaiah is glorious from the standpoint of literature alone. The swing of its majestic prose comforts the heart even while we read of doom. As we read, however, we wonder. Terrible as are these pictures of destruction, death, fear, hunger, and anguish, are they any worse than the things that have actually come upon the earth? Are they any worse than the destruction that we ourselves at this moment are raining upon Vietnam, so that men, women, and children of both North and South are burned, maimed, and killed?

It may be well, therefore, that we read Isaiah's be-wailings of the misery and destruction that shall come upon the earth, for we too need to be convicted of the sin and sickness of our nation. Conviction alone, how-ever, leads to despair. So here is the greater purpose of God speaking through Isaiah to the Israelites and to us: that this prophesied doom may be averted or mitigated. Prophecies of destruction contain or imply the word "if." If the people do not change, then these things will happen. If the people will repent and turn unto the Lord, then these things will not happen.

There are two ways, therefore, in which we who are supposed to be the sons of God may work toward miti-gating or averting the prophesied disasters of our time. One is the way of praying for the land, as Abraham did for Sodom and Gomorrah (Gen. 18:23ff.) and as the priests did yearly for the sins of the people. (Lev. 16:29-34; Heb. 9:7) The other is the way of speaking forth. We are not called to be prophets in Isaiah's exact pattern, and for this we praise God! Few of us would care to walk the earth naked and barefoot in order to attract people's attention. (Isa. 20:2-3) Nevertheless, there are ways in which we should testify to God's righteousness and to our need of reform, and we who are supposed to be Christians should know them. We should support and do and teach the truth, namely, that if we as a nation keep God's laws, upon which this nation was supposedly founded, we will survive and become great, and if we do not, we will be destroyed.

Isaiah must have wondered how the power of God *could* forgive when people would not hear and would not repent. He must have said, "Oh Lord, how can this be?" He must have listened with all his heart and with all his soul. And so, as he listened, there came to him little by little, fragment upon fragment, the glimpses of how this would be: that God Himself would come upon the earth in human form, that a virgin would give birth to a child and would call His name Emmanuel, meaning "God with us," and that through Him all the nations of the world would be blessed.

Thus we have these marvelous prophecies: "For unto us a child is born, unto us a son is given: and the government shall be upon his shoulder: and his name shall be called Wonderful, Counsellor, The mighty God, The everlasting Father, the Prince of Peace." (Isa. 9:6)

"And there shall come forth a rod out of the stem of Jesse, and a Branch shall grow out of his roots: and the spirit of the Lord shall rest upon him, the spirit of wisdom and understanding, the spirit of counsel and might, the spirit of knowledge and of the fear of the Lord." (Isa. 11:1-2)

"And a man shall be as an hiding place from the wind, and a covert from the tempest; as rivers of water in a dry place, as the shadow of a great rock in a weary land. And the eyes of them that see shall not be dim, and the ears of them that hear shall hearken." (Isa. 32:2-3)

"Say to them that are of a fearful heart, Be strong, fear not: behold, your God will come with vengeance, even God with a recompence; he will come and save you. Then the eyes of the blind shall be opened, and the ears of the deaf shall be unstopped. Then shall the lame man leap as an hart, and the tongue of the dumb sing: for in the wilderness shall waters break out, and streams in the desert." (Isa. 35: 4-6)

God came to earth in the form of a man, and Isaiah, His servant, saw Him centuries beforehand. Why not? When we live in the part of ourselves that is the spirit, we are living beyond space, beyond time. Upon earth Isaiah was contained in one physical body, operating through one brain. In the heavens Isaiah was an ever-living being only temporarily and partially abiding in a tabernacle of flesh. Isaiah saw and knew, therefore, that God would come to the earth in the form of a man. He came into our violence and hatred, and into the stupid fury of mankind. For among all living creatures, only mankind and the dove make fatal war against their own. Bees and wasps have more charity than man; birds and bats have more common sense than man. Lions and wolves and the wildest of wild creatures kill for food but not for personal enmity. Angry dogs forgive the vanquished, when man does not. The naturalist, Konrad Lorenz, says in his book *King Solomon's Ring* that dogs fight furiously, but when the vanquished is at the mercy of the victor, he stands in an attitude of complete submission, turns his head, and exposes his jugular vein, and his enemy cannot hurt him.

"But I say unto you, That ye resist not evil: but whosoever shall smite thee on thy right cheek, turn to him the other also," Jesus said. (Matt. 5:39) He not only said it, but He did it, and the power generated by His forgiveness flows on through all the agony of the centuries. He came, therefore, that all the nations of the world should be blessed. Perhaps Isaiah leaped to the ultimate purpose and the final outcome of this changing of the species of man by transplanting into him the Spirit of Christ. Perhaps he saw the kingdom of heaven, when the lion should eat straw like the ox, and the sucking child should play on the hole of the asp, and they should not hurt or destroy each other any more. (Isa. 11:6-9) Isaiah may, in other words, have seen through the regeneration of man to the kingdom of heaven, for when man walks the earth as the son of God, then surely he will make of this earth the footstool to heaven instead of an anteroom to hell.

Even before Jesus came, there were those among the Hebrews who did indeed walk the earth as the sons of God: Abraham, and Moses, and Elijah, and the glorious company of the prophets. Read Hebrews, Chapter II. Look upon those who moved by faith, and rejoice. After Jesus came, these same children of Abraham, now called the Jews, brought forth even greater heroes of the faith—Peter, the rock; Paul, the missionary; John, the great interpreter of Christ; Mary, the mother of Jesus.

Where have they gone? We, the Gentiles, are grafted on to this ancient root of God's theocracy. Some say that the blood of the chosen people of God runs in our veins, along with the blood of the Saxons and Normans, the Angles and Celts; that the ten tribes who were taken away into captivity and lost, found their way into the north countries. This may well be so. But there remain the brothers and sisters of Jesus Christ, the descendants of Judah and Benjamin whom we call the Jews. Has the scepter departed from them forever? What of the prophecies concerning these very lost tribes, prophecies that occur again and again both in the Old Testament and in the New Testament? In Jeremiah 23:7-8 we read: "Behold, the days come, saith the Lord, that they shall no more say, The Lord liveth, which brought up the children of Israel out of the land of Egypt; but, The Lord liveth, which brought up and which led the seed of the house of Israel out of the north country, and from all counties whither I had driven them; and they shall dwell in their own land."

How strange that we read these prophecies and pay no attention to them whatsoever! We shout aloud in our services on Easter and every holy day concerning the redemption of Israel, and we naïvely assume that we are Israel, or, rather, that the promises no longer apply to the Jews, neither to the lost ten tribes nor to the saved two tribes, but that they apply only to Christians. I wonder if this assumption can possibly have any truth in it.

"Fear not: for I am with thee," saith the Lord to the children of Israel. "I will bring thy seed from the east, and gather thee from the west; I will say to the north, Give up; and to the south, Keep not back: bring my sons from far, and my daughters from the ends of the earth: even every one that is called by my name: for I have created him for my glory, I have formed him; yea, I have made him." (Isa. 43:5-7) And in Isaiah 45:25

we read, "In the Lord shall all the seed of Israel be justified, and shall glory."

In Isaiah 49:13-16 we read this most touching word of compassion and love: "Sing, O heavens; and be joyful, O earth; and break forth into singing, O mountains: for the Lord hath comforted his people, and will have mercy upon his afflicted. But Zion said, The Lord hath forsaken me, and my Lord hath forgotten me. Can a woman forget her sucking child, that she should not have compassion on the son of her womb? Yea, they may forget, yet will I not forget thee. Behold, I have graven thee upon the palms of my hands; thy walls are continually before me."

We Gentiles who are Christians and are therefore "grafted on" to the root of Judaism are apt to think rather casually that these tender promises apply only to us, and that they have nothing to do with the Jews who to this day read them in their synagogues and await their fulfillment. Since we are grafted on, we have a right to believe that we also are graven upon the palms of His hands and that the walls of our salvation are continually before Him. But since we are grafted on, surely we should know that these promises refer also to the root upon which we are grafted, and that without them we cannot be completely saved from wars and troubles, any more than a plant can be completely whole without the wholeness of its roots. Some of the life of the root has come into us, yes. Not only have we absorbed the healing power of the Bible and its teaching but also quite likely the very blood of the ten tribes is mingled with our blood. Some of the life of a root comes into the branches and mingles with their life. But the fact remains that unless the whole of the root is fed with life, the plant remains weak and spindly.

If one studies all the words of the Bible, one will not find anywhere that God has utterly cut off and forgotten that nation that He chose to be a trial nation in which to work out His theocracy. I believe this not only because it is written in the Bible; I believe it also because in my own small experience with Jewish people I have found that there is still within many of them a great spiritual sensitivity and spiritual capacity.

People differ. We are not all made after the same pattern. Races differ; they have certain prevailing characteristics, and this we know perfectly well when we study the laws of life, although we continually deny it. We cling to the ridiculous concept that if only everybody in the world had public school education and electric refrigerators, they would all be the same. But no power on earth can make them the same, for they are different. God chose the Jewish people from all the races of the earth. We are apt to say to ourselves smugly that they were a small people, despised, outcast. We do not usually remind ourselves that they were and are a people superior in wisdom, superior in ability to earn and to manage money, and most of all superior in spiritual capacities.

For instance, there was a time years ago when a friend asked me to pray for a Jewish man violently ill with pneumonia. My friend told the man's wife that at such a time we would pray for her husband, Solomon, and she was to go and sit beside him at that time and be an open channel for our prayers. The next day she called up my friend, utterly and absolutely amazed. She said that as she sat beside him, the room was filled with light, and that her husband was instantly healed.

In my little book *Oh, Watchman* I have told the story of a Jewish man who is at the present time a Christian psychologist and of his healing, not only of his healing but of his instantaneous and immediate grasp of the nature and power of God, and even of his preknowledge concerning Jesus Christ.

There are many other stories that I could tell. For instance, there was a young Jewish mother whose first son was born with an incurable disease. A friend asked her husband whether he would be willing for me to go to the hospital and pray for the baby. This was a hard decision for him to make, but because it was his only son he finally agreed. I will never forget it. The two grandmothers stood by the door, both weeping. The little mother was frozen with fear, but as she sat, as beautiful as a rose, holding the child and unable to speak in her shyness and embarrassment, I laid my hands upon the baby and prayed for healing, and knew that it was taking place. Twelve years later I had a letter from this mother. She said, "Perhaps you have forgotten when you prayed for my son and he was healed. Next month is his Bar Mitzvah. I would like to invite you to be my guest during this time." Her letter moved me not only to joy but to sorrow and repentance for myself and for the church. Here are brothers and sisters of Jesus Christ, for whom He besought our love and compassion (Matt. 25:40) and how few of us ever think to go and heal them by His power!

God said through Isaiah, "Yea, they may forget, yet will I not forget thee." (Isa. 49:15) We may have forgotten His brethren, the Jews, but He has not forgotten. In Isaiah 51:3, we read: "For the Lord shall comfort Zion: he will comfort all her waste places; and he will make her wilderness like Eden, and her desert like the garden of the Lord; joy and gladness shall be found therein, thanksgiving, and the voice of melody."

And in Chapter 52:7, Isaiah wrote: "How beautiful upon the mountains are the feet of him that bringeth good tidings, that publisheth peace; that bringeth good tidings of good, that publisheth salvation; that saith unto Zion, Thy God reigneth!" We quote this continually, totally ignoring the words "that saith *unto Zion*, Thy God reigneth!" When I went into the hospital to pray for the little Jewish baby, perhaps I was saying unto Zion, "Thy God reigneth!" For I did pray in the name of God and through the power of God, and the mother and all her family saw that the Lord God still has power.

Most of us have little faith in the promises of the Bible. We may read them, but we simply do not believe them, and yet listen to what the Lord said in Isaiah 55:10-11 concerning these promises: "For as the rain cometh down, and the snow from heaven, and returneth not thither, but watereth the earth, and maketh it bring

forth and bud, that it may give seed to the sower, and
bread to the eater: so shall my word be that goeth forth
out of my mouth: it shall not return unto me void, but
it shall accomplish that which I please, and it shall prosper in the thing whereto I sent it."

Read the whole chapter; indeed read the whole book
of Isaiah, and take note: these promises were made to
the seed of Abraham, to the root of Jesse upon which
we are grafted. These promises have not been fulfilled.
Why? They are waiting for us. Jesus came to fulfill the
promises, and how can we expect the Jewish people,
the original inheritors of the promises, to accept Jesus
Christ when they cannot accept us who are named with
the name of Christ? And how can they accept us when
we do not accept them? When Jesus came on earth, He
came to the Jews. Certain Jews accepted Him: James,
John, Peter, Paul, and countless others. They accepted
Him under threat of death and persecution. They accepted Him even when they knew they might be thrown
to the lions. Others did not accept Him.

No, some did not accept Him, but God, says Isaiah,
will not rest or be satisfied until they are gathered together from the far ends of the earth and brought back
to Him (Isa. 60:1ff.) Who is to bring them back to Him?
Through whom are the words of Jesus, our Lord, to be
spoken nowadays? Through whom are the works of
Jesus, our Lord, now to be done? Read John 14:12:
"Verily, verily, I say unto you, He that believeth on me,
the works that I do shall he do also; and greater works
than these shall he do; because I go unto my Father."
Jesus no longer comes in *one* body of flesh, but He
comes in many bodies of flesh. He expects us to carry
on His work. Therefore, for whom is He waiting? He is
waiting for us.

How shall we carry on His work, and how shall we
bring the message of the power of God through Jesus
Christ to these His brethren? He told us! He said,
"Verily I say unto you, Inasmuch as ye have done it unto
one of the least of these my brethren, ye have done it
unto me." (Matt. 25:40) First of all, then, by kindness.

First of all, by love and compassion, and following that, by showing forth His great and mighty works. This is the very thing that we have not done. We are continually moaning and worrying about the branch that is grafted on. We concern ourselves about the church, and the deadness of the church, the coldness of the church, the lack of power of the church. We concern ourselves rightly, but we forget that this church is *grafted on.* We are like a farmer who tends the branches of a tree, sprays it carefully to keep off bugs, picks off every withered leaf, watches over it and broods over it with anxiety, but never feeds the roots of the tree. Of course the branches become dead!

If the Bible is true, then I do not see how we can ignore this fact, that the church of Christ will never be completely filled with the power of the Holy Spirit until the roots are fed, until the graft is healed, until the love of Jesus Christ in some fashion reaches those for whom it was first sent forth, those among whom He Himself lived and worked, those among whom He Himself was born: the Jews. And surely the greatest work of Satan is the keeping alive of enmity between Christian and Jew, so that rather than feeding these roots with the love of Christ, watering them with the fresh water of the power of God, it seems as if Christendom through all the ages has done its very best to kill these roots, both figuratively and also, to our shame and horror, literally. Surely of all the sins that Christian people have committed against God, this is the greatest.

Perhaps you are thinking, "But *I* haven't." Have you not? Are you not part of the whole body of Christ, the church? Then do you not share in the great crimes against these people that have been committed in gas chambers, in torture rooms, on execution grounds? Do not all of us share in this? We need to recognize this fact so that we can repent for it. Repenting, at least we can do our very best to atone by showing personal kindness and consideration and love to those Jewish people who live in our midst. "How beautiful upon the mountains are the feet of him that bringeth good tidings, that publisheth peace." (Isa. 52:7)

10
Ezekiel

✳

We live in a physical world that we can see, and up to a point can understand. We live also at the same time in a spiritual world of such terrifying dimensions that for the most part we cannot see it, and that is to our comfort. And yet from time to time there have been people who have been able to see that world. From the very beginning this has been so, as we remember in our studies. However even Adam, even Moses, even Abraham could not see the glory of God and the world that is beyond this world with such awful clarity as did the prophet Ezekiel, who was also a priest.

Unless we realize that he was seeing with the spiritual eyes into the fourth dimension and dimensions beyond, then the book of Ezekiel seems to us utterly beyond understanding. For instance, in the very beginning the prophet Ezekiel saw a vision of the glory of God that laid him on the ground in terror and awe and physical weakness. (Ezek. 1) He looked up and beheld in the sky unidentified flying objects; some of them seemed alive, and he called them living creatures. He tried to describe them. The descriptions make no sense to us because they were of a type of life that we cannot even begin to comprehend. Beside the living creatures, proceeding along with them in their lightning flashes across the skies—for they moved from horizon to horizon in ⸍er of seconds—he saw other objects which he ⸍ as wheels, full of eyes within and without. ⸍at these objects were energized by the living ⸍hat went beside them.

Now what did Ezekiel see? Could it possibly have any relation whatsoever to the unidentified flying objects that many people of today have seen, even I? In Chapter 7 I mentioned an incident which was certainly not a "vision," nor was my spirit edified by the aroma of garbage! Nevertheless, as I rounded the corner of the garage and lifted the lid of the garbage-can, I saw popping over the little hill behind the house an unidentified flying object. It appeared to be some four feet in diameter. In the center it glowed like a fire burning low. This dull orange faded out into cream at the object's fuzzy edges.

As I glanced there came another and another. I counted altogether twenty-eight, some in twos and threes, and occasionally a single one, flashing from horizon to horizon in about three seconds. They moved in a zigzag flight, something like dragonflies upon the top of a lake. "And they turned not when they went." (Ezek. 1:12) Now I, of course, have no idea what these were, nor where they come from, and yet I did feel that they were not indwelt by living beings but that they were energized by a living intelligence perhaps residing in some other unidentified flying object which I was unable to see. These things were absolutely unquestionably real. I was perfectly cool and in my right mind, and I took the empty garbage container, carried it back to the house, and said nothing at the time about this. It thrilled me greatly that I was glimpsing something beyond one's ordinary human sight, even though I saw it with my human eyes, wide open and wide awake—something mysterious, something strange, something rather wonderful. Whether it was from the spiritual world, or whether it was the appearance of some sort of intelligence emanating from some other place in this created universe, I have no idea, but it was a thing of wonder and I did not wish to speak of it, lest its numinous quality be dimmed by words.

The prophet Ezekiel was seeing high up and far away, beyond anything that I saw. What he saw I do not know, and yet I thank God for every vision that one sees of life beyond this earth. One of these days we must live in the life beyond this earth. How much easier it will be if we have already caught glimpses here and there of things beyond our understanding!

Upon seeing these weird and inexplicable things, the prophet Ezekiel fell on his face. The Lord said to him, "Son of man, stand upon thy feet, and I will speak unto thee." (Ezek. 2:1) Many a sermon could be preached upon this. We are not supposed to grovel before the Lord. He created us living beings in His own image and His own likeness. He respects these little creatures that he has made upon the earth. He talks to us as we stand upon our feet and listen in holy fear but not in abject terror.

So Ezekiel listened and God gave him a strange and sad prophecy concerning the children of Israel. He told Ezekiel, even as He had told Isaiah, that these people would not keep His commandments, and that they would therefore suffer great tribulation and be scattered into all countries upon the face of the earth. Nevertheless, He commanded the prophet to speak it forth.

Why? The first reason, the one that He gave Ezekiel, was very simple: if the prophet warned them, then at least his conscience was clear. He had done his duty; it would not be held against him if they did not obey. Have our prophets forgotten this today? Have our priests forgotten this? Have the ministers of the gospel of Christ forgotten?

Some years ago there was an article in a popular magazine entitled, "A Little Brimstone, Please," saying that ministers have a right and a duty to tell people what is evil and what is good. Even if none heed him, the minister himself is held blameless if he had warned them. However, the time will be, as even Ezekiel saw later in a vision that perhaps he did not at the time fully understand, when the seeds planted in the deep mind of the race will bring among peoples and nations a new birth and a new awareness. Similarly, even though at the time it may seem that no one heeds us, yet was are commanded to endeavor in every way we know to open men's eyes to the reality of God and man and time and eternity: to open their eyes in ways that will give them hope and courage, not in ways that will lead them only to sit down and condemn themselves mournfully to extinction.

When the Lord thus appeared to Ezekiel, as He did more than once, the appearance brought him to his knees, and brought him to his face, not only because of a feeling of awe but because of physical weakness. After one of these visions he sat astonished, overcome with amazement, for seven days. (Ezek. 3:15) How perfectly fantastic! Or is it so fantastic? We read of this same kind of thing time and again in the Bible. We remember the vision of St. Paul when he saw the living Christ, how he fell on the ground and lay as one dead, and how the light of that vision blinded him so that for a while he could see nothing. (Acts 9:1-18) He had seen more than his human body was quite able to endure, that is all. We remember also the tenderness with which the Lord sent to him a Christian, a man named Ananias, to console him and to pray for him, and to fill him with the Holy Spirit.

So it was with Ezekiel. The Lord did not send him a human friend; there was no human friend. But as the Spirit of the Lord lifted him up and stood him upon his feet, then the Spirit of the Lord Himself entered into him. He perceived the Lord; he sensed an emanation from the Being of God and from that time forth he arose and went forth and obeyed the Lord. (Ezek. 2:2)

Is this so strange? By no means! This kind of thing has happened time and again in a smaller way to ministers and other prophets whom the Lord has called. Just recently I went to a testimonial dinner given for a hospital chaplain, and he was asked in the "This Is Your Life" program, "Why did you enter the ministry?" He said that one night as he was going to bed something moved within him, and he wondered what life was all about, and what he intended to do in the world. So great was the wondering that he sat on the side of his bed with one sock in his hand all night long, and when morning came he found himself still sitting there holding the sock. Then he heard himself saying aloud, "All right, Lord, I'll be a minister." He did not know with the conscious mind what he saw and heard in that long night, but something moved him. And he arose and followed.

This small story could be repeated again and again and again. We find like instances, and far more spectacular than this, in the lives of the great evangelists. The Spirit of the Lord moved upon them; the Spirit of the Lord called them and set them on their feet. The Spirit of the Lord said, "Go forth!"

The prophet Ezekiel had a very high tolerance for the Spirit of the Lord; there is no question about that. The things that the Lord showed him, and the things that the Lord told him, were astonishing and some of them were hard to take. He was called upon to be an evangelist, indeed a very spectacular evangelist. He was commanded to perform symbolic actions, some of them seemingly absurd and some of them rather revolting, as when he was told to eat only certain most unappetizing foods, even prepared with dung as fuel. (Ezek. 4:12) These things he was to do to draw attention to himself, so that people would say, "What a strange man! He must be a holy man of God!"

How can we account for the physical effect of these visions upon the prophet Ezekiel so that he fell unconscious, or fainted? This is not beyond comprehension. I know from my own experience that to pray with the whole heart and mind and spirit takes tremendous energy. There are some who say that prayer is restful. To me it is not restful. It is the most strenuous of activities. Real prayer, prayer in which one becomes filled with the Lord's spiritual power, takes energy. I have never fallen on my face as one dead, but I have indeed felt after such a time of prayer that I was utterly wrung dry of all strength, both spiritual and physical. After a healing service I have felt sometimes that I could hardly move, that I was not myself, that all that was really me was drawn out of me and the very essence of life in me was weakened.

A certain lady I know has an inborn capacity for visions, a great spiritual sensitivity. One day on the way to work, light burst upon her; she saw it with her eyes, she saw it with everything in her. It was so blinding and so intense that she stumbled and fell. Arising again, she found herself almost too weak to walk. She crept uncertainly, feeling her way because she could hardly see, to the office where she worked, and there collapsed upon a sofa. She was taken to a hospital and given every possible test and examination. Her blood pressure was exceedingly low; it seemed to the doctors that she must have had a heart attack, and yet there was no real evidence of heart trouble. They kept her in the hospital and gave her all kinds of medication, and she became worse and worse because they were unwittingly tampering with the effort of the Spirit to move within her.

Fortunately, by the grace of God, she had a minister who understood those things. May the time come when all of our ministers will understand not only Hebrew and Greek and the history of the church, but will also understand the souls of men, the delicate make-up of the spirit and mind and body of human beings, so that they can really minister to them. This minister explained what was really happening within her spirit in a deeper and more psychological way than I can explain it. Therefore, she arose in her courage, refused further medication, left the hospital, and went home. In a very short time she was totally restored to a balance of spirit, mind, and body, and she went forth radiant with new life.

This same minister told me that there are people in mental institutions today because they have had spiritual experiences that no one could explain. They did not know how to incorporate these experiences of the unconscious into their total life and personality. "My people are destroyed for lack of knowledge," so we read in Hosea 4:6.

Most of us, you and I, are not, as the above-mentioned minister is, deeply versed in psychology, and in the lives of the church fathers, and in the mysticism of the saints. Most of us are armed, perhaps rather feebly, only with a modicum of common sense. But if we admit that the spiritual kingdom is real, and that a part of us lives in this greater awareness, surely then we can accept the fact that a life beyond can impinge upon us. And if it leaves us temporarily shaken or weak, that is good. It is simply because the Holy Spirit of God has accomplished a bit of an operation deep down, below the level of our understanding. All we need to do is to give God time to finish His work in the unconscious. Ezekiel sat as one astonished and said not a word for seven days. We will not perhaps have to go as far as that, but at least we can keep an experience within the privacy of our own minds until it has been incorporated into the total being.

There is one particular vision of Ezekiel upon which I should like to comment in some detail, because it is tremendous and fascinating. Ezekiel says, "The hand of the Lord was upon me, and carried me out in the spirit of the Lord, and set me down in the midst of the valley which was full of bones." (Ezek. 37:1)

What did he mean by that? He could have meant simply that through the working of the Lord a truth was being revealed to him in a symbolic or pictorial fashion. He might have meant that his spirit merged into the Spirit of the Lord, and that his spirit therefore was temporarily carried beyond his body, and set down in a valley that was full of bones. Through this valley full of bones he was given a vision that opened his eyes to a new understanding. "And, behold, there were very many in the open valley; and, lo, they were very dry. And he said unto me, Son of man, can these bones live? And I answered, O Lord God, thou knowest. Again he said unto me, Prophesy upon these bones, and say unto them, O ye dry bones, hear the word of the Lord. Thus saith the Lord God unto these bones; Behold, I will cause breath to enter into you, and ye shall live: and I will lay sinews upon you, and will bring up flesh upon you, and cover you with skin, and put breath in you, and ye shall live; and ye shall know that I am the Lord. So I prophesied as I was commanded," said Ezekiel, "and as I prophesied, there was a noise, and behold a shaking, and the bones came together, bone to his bone. And when I beheld, lo, the sinews and the flesh came upon them, and the skin covered them above: but there was no breath in them." (Ezek. 37:2-8)

The symbolism of this passage seems to me amusingly and tragically clear, for indeed through many centuries there has been a valley full of bones, and they are very dry. I have heard sermon after sermon pointing out the bony structure of the church, pointing out the skeleton of theology. And behold, it is very dry! Then the church authorities become uncomfortably aware of the dryness, and behold there is a noise and a shaking, and the bones come together, bone to his bone, committee unto committee, subcommittee unto subcommittee, convocation unto convocation, implementing this and considering that, adding project to project and venture to venture. But there is not the breath of the Holy Spirit in them; there is therefore no life in them. This does not mean they are not good. It is good that the bones be assembled together in some sort of shape, ready to receive life when it does come. Life cannot be breathed into a pile of bones that have no shape and form. If the bones are fitted together, they make a framework for life. But alas, too often the implementing and the planning end with the fitting of the bones together.

I once heard a bishop's letter read in church. It began with a great proclamation of the fact that in order for the church really to live it was necessary that we should have the power of the Holy Spirit in us. And I thought, "Oh praise God, the bishop has caught it!" Then the letter went on to state that the method by which we were to attain new life within us was a system of uniting diocese to diocese, bone joining together unto his bone; and we were to enter into a certain financial relationship with a faraway bishop. No doubt this was good, but there was no breath in it. I have not noticed the Holy Spirit entering and shaking the church because of a financial alliance between two dioceses.

What is it then that can really awaken a church? Ezekiel gives us the answer. "Then said he unto me, Prophesy unto the wind, prophesy, son of man, and say to the wind, Thus saith the Lord God; Come from the four winds, O breath, and breathe upon these slain, that they may live. So I prophesied as he commanded me, and the breath came into them, and they lived, and stood up upon their feet, an exceeding great army." (Ezek. 37:9-10)

The word "wind" (*ruach*) in the Old Testament is the same as the word for "breath," which word is used to mean the breath of God, the Holy Spirit. Now you see the meaning of Ezekiel's vision! It is good for bone to be fitted to his bone. It is good for the organizations of the church to be neatly fitted together. It is good for the expenses of these organizations to be covered by what might be called the "flesh" of finance. It is good for the skin of a new church building and a new parish house, and whatever equipment is needed, to cover these bones. But there is no life in them until they are filled with the Spirit of God.

Of course we are inclined to take for granted that the Spirit of God does fill them. Herein we make a great mistake. Anybody knows a live body from a dead body; anybody can tell a living human being from a corpse. Can everybody tell a live church from a dead church? I can tell, taking note of my own feelings. When I enter some churches, my heart lifts up. I feel therein a sense of joy, a radiation of life, an awareness of the presence of God.

I will never forget entering Christ Church, St. Lawrence, in Sydney, Australia. Although the churchmanship was different from the broad and simple worship to which I was accustomed, although the place was full of the odor of incense, and candles glimmered faintly through the haze, although the ministers and all the acolytes marched in glorious procession around the church sprinkling holy water—nevertheless, or perhaps because, or perhaps through these bones, these contrivances, the Spirit of God in that place was full of glory and full of light. Why? Because the rector of that church, Father John Hope, for thirty-five years had gathered in the lonely and the desperate, had saved the lost and had healed the sick, believing in the power of God. The work of God was done in that church through the power of the Holy Spirit. Therefore even the building itself was filled with the life of God.

I have been in other churches and found there only coldness and emptiness. So have you, and let us not deny it. It is no good just saying, "Well, it is a church, and therefore the Spirit of God is there." That is just the same as looking at a corpse and saying, "That is a body, and so therefore life is there." Now the power of God, His healing light, either is there or is not there. I have been in churches in which the ministers were cold and critical, turning up their noses at the power of God, denying categorically that Jesus Christ is able to do miracles today—and there was no life in those churches.

My heart goes out to the faithful members who do not leave such churches, but stay and endeavor to bring them to life. For there is this difference between a dead church and a dead body: it is much easier to bring a dead church to life than to bring a dead body to life. I do not say that it is impossible to bring a dead body to life. Recently I heard from Tommy Tyson of a great revival in Indonesia in which there were nine resurrections of dead people, yet I have never seen one with my eyes, and I would think it a somewhat difficult procedure. I hope if the Lord ever called me to try such a thing that I would be ready to listen and obey, but so far He knows that I do not have enough faith for this, and He has not called me.

To bring a church to life should not be too difficult.

So my heart goes out with thanksgiving to the humble little people who stay in their church though it be cold, though it be merely a highly organized collection of dead bones. I trust that those Christians will continue to pray in that church and for that church, that it may be filled with the power of God, so that those in need will find there His healing presence. For instance, I once knew a young man in great need of just this: the active power of God in a church. He did not belong to my husband's church but he came to me for prayer and was uplifted and strengthened and able to go forth and support himself and his family. Afterward he came every Sunday to this church, a strange one for him, and just sat in the back pew. "That way," he told me, "I get enough to hold me during the week." Then he was away for a month on a business trip. On returning he brought me the bulletins of four Episcopal churches in different cities. "I tried them all," he said wistfully, "and He wasn't there."

In one sense I know that the Lord *was* there. He was there but His hands were tied. Because of the lack of faith in those churches, He could not move. A young man came to church seeking help. He did not need extended counseling. He did not need a special service of healing with the laying-on of hands. All he needed was a regular, ordinary service of the church with enough faith pervading the place so that he could feel it. But it was not there.

"So I prophesied as he commanded me," said Ezekiel, "And the breath came into them, and they lived, and stood up upon their feet, an exceeding great army." (Ezek. 37:10) This can be. The Lord showed Ezekiel that in spite of all the trials and troubles and agony that would come to the world, the day would dawn when the Holy Spirit of God would enter into these dry bones and they would arise and stand upon their feet, a very great army.

In the next verse we read, "Son of man, these bones are the whole house of Israel: behold, they say, Our bones are dried, and our hope is lost: we are cut off for our parts. Therefore prophesy and say unto them, Thus saith the Lord God; Behold, O my people, I will open your graves, and cause you to come up out of your graves, and bring you into the land of Israel. And ye shall know that I am the Lord, when I have opened your graves, O my people, and brought you up out of your graves, and shall put my spirit in you, and ye shall live, and I shall place you in your own land." (Ezek. 37:11-14)

Here again we have the prophecy coming through Abraham and Isaac and Jacob, through Jeremiah and Isaiah and all the prophets. The Spirit of the Lord applied this vision not only to the church of that day but immediately and particularly to the whole house of Israel. These promises are very definite. The Lord will gather the children of Israel together from all the lands whither they have been driven, and will bring them again to their own place. When that time comes, they shall know that the Lord is God.

As we have seen, we are grafted onto the house of Israel, and the promise is for us as well as for them. Ezekiel was seeing farther than he knew. He was seeing the day when the Holy Spirit, promised by Jesus Christ, broke out upon the whole church so that they were filled with power and with joy. (Acts 2:1ff.) In an instant, in the twinkling of an eye, they were totally transformed. They entered that upper room trembling and uncertain human beings, blindly obeying a command that they did not understand: to wait there for the promise that Jesus had given them, the promise of the Comforter, the strength-giver, who would quicken them in joy and in power and in understanding. They went forth so filled with joy and so radiant in power that men, not understanding the intoxication of the Spirit, could only assume that they were drunk. They were totally transformed. They were completely different. And yet this new life had been from the beginning potentially in every one of them, each in his own way.

We may think of simple examples of this kind of

transformation, such as popcorn blossoming into a new form which was, nevertheless, contained in the old hard kernel, or a butterfly emerging from a cocoon, a winged creature full of beauty, yet that new beauty was potentially in the ugly worm that made the cocoon. Did God prepare the popcorn and the butterfly in order to show us even in these simple forms of life the exploding power of the Creator?

Alas, after Pentecost the power slowly faded; the life dwindled away. The old enemy worked through the mind of man to discard the very source of life that had made the church a "very great army." The soldiers of that army laid down their banners of faith and took instead the veil of rationalism. Behind this veil they hid again from God, as Adam and Eve hid in the Garden of Eden. (Gen. 3:8)

Now the veil is being torn away. Science has taken from us the smug excuse that we need not believe in anything that we cannot see. Who has ever seen an atom? Or an electron? Or even a DNA molecule? Who has ever seen pure energy, or the actual flow of the vibration that makes electricity? Yet we see electricity as it shines in our lamps. We perceive the moving of energy as it causes our cars to roar over the highway. We cannot even see the wind, but we know the wind blows when we see the dead leaves flying before it. We are not required to know the historical Edison to believe in his power. We know the power because we can turn on our lights and see it.

Many people refuse to believe in the historical Jesus, while others deliver learned lectures and write heavy tomes to prove that He did exist. But the simplest way to know the truth of Him and of His Holy Spirit is simply to turn on the power by faith and see it shine. Ezekiel saw it ages and ages ago in a vision. The breath of God (the Holy Spirit) breathed upon the dry bones, and they stood upon their feet and lived, a very great army.

In our day, dry bones are beginning to live again. The army is advancing. The light is beginning to shine into a dark world. The power given by the Holy Spirit of Jesus Christ is moving upon those who are near and upon those who are far away. And that power shall live and shall move until, "The earth shall be filled with the knowledge of the glory of the Lord, as the waters cover the sea." (Hab. 2:14)

11
Wine and a Fig Tree

✳

As we have seen in studying the Old Testament, God the Creator tried to make Himself known to the human beings whom He had set in motion upon the earth. In the beginning they saw and heard Him clearly, for the limited and dark thinking of evil had not yet shrouded Him. But as we have seen in an earlier chapter they separated themselves from Him by overambition and rebellion and they lost their "bright nature": the capacity to see Him. Therefore He tried to show Himself to them in signs and wonders: for instance, in a burning bush (Exod. 3:2), in food from the skies (Exod. 16:13-14), and in water out of a rock. (Num. 20:7-11) But their glimpses of His reality were ephemeral, and the veil remained. Again He showed Himself to Moses in a mountain shaking and afire with power (Exod. 20:18), and later on His glory lurked in an "ark of the covenant" so charged with holy energy that an ordinary man could not touch it without dropping dead (2 Sam. 6:6-7), as one cannot touch a live wire heavily charged with electricity without dropping dead.

These methods proved too dangerous. But God still desired to bring forth sons: living beings who might know Him, partake of His power, and administer it upon the earth. (John 1:12) Therefore, in the fullness of time He came veiled in flesh, His power stepped down into a human wave-length. He compressed His glory into an unbelievably small compass and set in motion the life process in the Virgin Mary without the cooperation of a human father. This was a small miracle compared to the miracle of creating on earth the process of birth in the beginning—a miracle so common that we no longer wonder at it.

He came in straw and amid the smell of dung in the stables of an inn, with no permanent abiding place. He comes anew each Christmastide in tinsel and, all too often, amid the smell of tobacco and gay parties that for Him can be no permanent abiding place. Yet lights are lit for Him all over the land, blossoming here in California in crimson and gold over the dark foothills. The innkeepers did not know the meaning of His coming, but the angels knew and so did a few stray shepherds and wise men from afar—only a handful from among earth's millions. Most people do not really know today why the soft lights of Christmas enfold the sprawling cities in a rosy glow. The angels know and so do a few stray laborers in His vineyard, the earth, and a very, very few wise men from afar. But even to the unknowing multitudes the lights of His coming make a shining above the sordidness of the earthly habitations wherein we live. It is His will that the light shall shine, not only above but also within every soul, transmuting death into life, and making men truly the sons of God.

This man from God who was God once said, "I have a baptism to be baptised with; and how am I straitened till it be accomplished!" (Luke 12:50) How He was straitened! How He was tied as in a straitjacket—the strait-jacket of flesh! His sacrifice did not begin at Calvary nor yet at Gethsemane but when He realized that He must veil His glory and function within the narrow confines of the flesh. So instead of a flash of fire that might either destroy or recreate the earth, He sent forth only small flashes of light to little people here and there, teaching and healing them in a way that they could at least begin to understand. He did not begin even this humble service until He was thirty years old. He returned from Jerusalem with His parents at the age of twelve and was subject to them in their home. We assume that He worked in His father's

carpenter shop as a young man. Legends which have
grown up around Him, however, include stories dating
from the fifth century of His visiting England, to
modern wonderings as to His having been an Essene.
Who knows? The earth is wide and the waters thereof
are great. He might indeed have crossed the waters to
far places or He might have studied beside the Dead
Sea in a holy group which we might call a seminary
or a monastery. The area of His life hidden from us is
greater than the area revealed to us and perhaps there
is a reason for this hiding, just as there is a reason for
the revealing.

When He emerges again into our sight He emerges
as a human being instinct with a divine life, even as
He said we should also be instinct with this light of God
that is life. (Matt. 5:14-16) There were those who
sensed this light and came to Him for healing, and He
healed all who came. The question why He healed
diseases does not appear in the Bible. There is no question, any more than there is a question why light shines
into a room when we open a window into sunlight.
There were those, as at the pool of Bethesda, who did
not ask Him for healing. Only occasionally did He
seek out one of these and say, "Wilt thou be made
whole?" (John 5:6) But those who opened a window
by coming to Him, He never turned away. Moreover
in His disconcerting fashion He said that those who
believe in Him should do the works that He did. (John
14:12) The question of the ages is: Why do we not
do them? And why, even when we try to heal by faith,
do we so often fail? I have endeavored to answer this
in my book *The Healing Light.*

The fact is that all the reasons for our failures, and
for our imperfect triumphs in prayer, would fill many
books. One of the primary reasons may be simply that
we have not understood that the light that heals is a
real energy, the same creative energy from which all
worlds were made: the original light of God. Not understanding this, we have been too inclined to think in
terms of magic—of God like a capricious monarch

passing a miracle from time to time in a whimsical and irrational manner—though of course we have not used those words but have mouthed pious phrases concerning "His mysterious will." There are indeed many mysteries concerning His will, just as there are many mysteries concerning the tremendous subject of light. But there are certain simple facts concerning light that we are able to understand: light is real, and when we open a window to it, light shines in.

I have often wondered why Jesus began His ministry with a miracle that was not a healing at all but involved a simple and trivial matter: a domestic emergency due to lack of wine. Could it have been to show that He, Jesus, was Lord of light itself: the creative energy from which all worlds are made?

The Creator did not do violence to the life of the bush when He showed His light within it. It was not consumed, and when the glory of God burned no more within it, the bush remained an ordinary bush. (Exod. 3:2) God did not alter the earthly material of the ark when He showed forth through it the Shekinah glory. (Exod. 40:35) It did not turn into gold or diamonds, but remained to all appearances simply an ark made of wood. In somewhat the same way God did not do violence to the human appearance or nature of Jesus Christ. He remained simply a man in appearance, no glory from beyond making Him conspicuous as Isaiah pointed out in prophecy long before He was born. (Isa. 53:2-3) His nature and being were those of a man, though the glory and the creative power of God worked through Him.

Long before there were any human beings, God had sent forth His Word, and by faith had created what we call matter, which is also energy: earth, and water, and the skies above them, and it is not too strange that the first public and recorded miracle of the Son of God should have concerned matter.

"There was a marriage in Cana of Galilee; and the mother of Jesus was there: and both Jesus was called, and His disciples, to the marriage. And when they wanted wine, the mother of Jesus saith unto Him, They have no wine." (John 2:1-3)

One wonders why did she speak to Him, and why did the servants report this domestic difficulty to the mother of Jesus. This was the first of His public miracles, and yet strange things must have happened before this, perhaps even in His childhood, so that He was known to have miraculous powers. Maybe in a time of need, loaves of bread appeared mysteriously in an earthen oven. And why not? For here was the one who, with God the Father and God the Holy Ghost, created the worlds in the beginning. (John 1:1-3) It would be strange indeed if power did not from time to time shine out through Him upon little matters of this earth.

"Jesus saith unto her, Woman, what have I to do with thee? mine hour is not yet come." (John 2:4) This sounds very strange to us, but apparently the term "woman" was not considered disrespectful in those days. However, He must have said this with a smile because His mother was not affronted. "Mine hour is not yet come," said He, but still she was not discouraged.

"His mother saith unto the servants, Whatsoever He saith unto you, do it. And there were set there six waterpots of stone, after the manner of the purifying of the Jews, containing two or three firkins apiece. [A firkin is three or four gallons.]

"Jesus saith unto them, Fill the waterpots with water. And they fiilled them up to the brim." (John 2:7) To fill the pots with water was not an easy matter. And just at this particular moment surely nobody needed all that water! What would have happened if they had refused to do as Jesus said? No miracle would have taken place. For in order for Jesus to answer the need of people it was necessary for Him to have their cooperation and obedience.

"And He saith unto them, Draw out now, and bear unto the governor of the feast. And they bare it." (John 2:8) The governor of a feast is a caterer, and more than a caterer. At my own wedding in China we had a governor of the feast. He not only supervised the kitchen, but also calculated the price of all the wedding presents so that the bridegroom could give the correct tip to those who brought them. Apparently at the wedding in Cana the governor of the feast also tasted the wine.

Now let us not be upset because they drank wine. Some people say it was unfermented; I do not know about that, but I know that in many a country wine is the natural thing to drink. The people did not have coffee nor tea; no one had as yet invented Coca-Cola. The proper drink was wine, and the quality of the wine seemed a matter of considerable importance to the host. The governor of the feast, therefore, had to taste this water from the well and decide on its virtue as wine. The servants knew this, yet they actually risked "losing face" and did this far-out deed. They drew out water, and in faith carried it to the governor of the feast.

"When the ruler of the feast had tasted the water that was made wine, and knew not whence it was: (but the servants which drew the water knew;) the governor of the feast called the bridegroom, and saith unto him. Every man at the beginning doth set forth good wine; and when men have well drunk, then that which is worse; but thou hast kept the good wine until now. This beginning of miracles did Jesus in Cana of Galilee, and manifested forth His glory; and His disciples believed on him." (John 2:9-11)

Now why did Jesus do this? He could have manifested His glory in healing someone who was sick, for instance. We would consider that just a little bit offbeat, but not quite as much so as changing water into wine! Why then. . . ?

First of all, I think He did it simply because He cared. He did not want to see the bridegroom's family upset and embarrassed because their refreshments ran out, any more than He would want us to be embarrassed and upset by such a mishap. In this as in all His miracles there are two aspects, reflections of His twofold nature: first, He acted out of love and concern for those particular people who were in front of His eyes. Second, He taught in a parable something that people far away down the path of time would someday understand. He proclaimed for us, right here in the beginning of His ministry, that He was not merely a good man, not merely a preacher and a teacher and a healer, but that He partook of the creative nature and power of God the Father. No one is like unto Him in heaven or earth. No one can be compared to Him. We can reflect a bit of His glory, so that in a sense we can also be called the sons of God, but we are the sons of God only through Him, as the sunshine lights the world through the sun. We have a bit of His nature in us, but the wholeness of the Godhead can never be in us as it was and is in Jesus Christ.

Let us not forget, therefore, that God is primarily a creator of material things: suns and planets and universes without end. We like to think of God as being "spiritual," but that does not fully explain His nature. He manifests and expresses His nature in the act of creation. Therefore His own being, His own light, His own energy, vibrates and flows in this created universe. The breath of God breathes through summer and winter, day and night, high tide and low tide, and in the deeper mysteries of which these are but little symbols.

My own spirit timidly grasped this long ago, and it comforted me greatly to read this same thought in the works of Pierre Teilhard de Chardin. Jesus was familiar with the nature of earth, air, and water, and He knew something that our most advanced men of science are just beginning to grasp: that what we call matter could just as truthfully be called energy. Though I can say this in words, I cannot really understand it. But Jesus was conversant with this energy. He knew exactly the pattern of the molecules of hydogen and oxygen put together to form water. Furthermore, being the Creator, He sensed and knew within Himself the method of changing these patterns so that the water could become wine.

Some people may say that at the wedding in Cana, which we are considering, Jesus did not really make water into wine. He merely caused the water to taste like wine. I would answer in our crude fashion of today, "So what?" To the governor of the feast, to the bridegroom and the guests, this was wine.

But why need we try to understand this rather fantastic miracle? Why not just dismiss it, as most people do, as a myth or a fairy tale?

First, to dismiss part of the Bible as false weakens our faith in the whole Bible and thus takes away its healing power. It is one thing to have honest doubts, and simply to lay a matter on the table, saying, "Well, I don't understand that, but some day I will." This keeps the mind open for an understanding that may come later. But to refuse to consider possibilities of truth in a Bible story prevents us from learning the hidden lessons stored up in these stories for future generations. . . . For remember, Jesus said that the works that He did we are to do also. (John 14:12)

Could we then by faith change the nature of water in any way whatsoever? Have you ever heard these words, "Sanctify this water to the mystical washing away of sin"? Yes, of course. In baptism. But does anything happen to the water? It does. An invisible spiritual energy enters into it. I have heard of scientific experiments showing a sort of light in the water after it has been blessed, but of course, not being a scientist, I cannot prove this. But I know of a certainty that a miracle-working power enters into the water when it is blessed for baptism, because of many instantaneous healings of babies baptized in emergency. In fact, the only miracle of resurrection in which I have personally had a small part happened in this way, as I have recounted at the end of Chapter 7.

I know, then, the possibility of the renewal of life in the body of an infant upon baptism. What the renewal of the life of the soul may be or the washing away of the inherited sins of the world, I do not know. But because Jesus manifested forth His power upon water in the sight of men, I dare to dream. . . .

Let us now consider another of these strange miracles of Jesus. "Now in the morning as he returned into the city, he hungered. And when he saw a fig tree in the way, he came to it, and found nothing thereon, but leaves only, and said unto it, Let no fruit grow on thee henceforward for ever. And presently the fig tree withered away." (Matt. 21:18-19)

St. Mark tells us this same story (Mark 11:12-14), and comments moreover that, "the time of figs was not yet." In other words, it was not the season for figs. What a strange thing, therefore, for Jesus to do! Was he merely angry with the fig tree, telling it to wither away because it had no figs, when it had no business to have figs anyway? This is indeed perplexing.

"And when the disciples saw it, they marvelled, saying, How soon is the fig tree withered away! Jesus answered and said unto them, Verily, I say unto you, If ye have faith, and doubt not, ye shall not only do this which is done to the fig tree, but also if ye shall say unto this mountain, Be thou removed, and be thou cast into the sea; it shall be done." (Matt. 21:20-21)

What a fantastic person to utter words like this and expect us to take them seriously! This has been for me one of the most difficult miracles to understand and to believe, and yet I have come to understand a bit of it.

There are times when a fig tree, even though its season is past, may have a few figs left upon it. At my summer home in New Hampshire, there are times when even though blueberries have long since ripened, a certain bush may still have some rather shriveled fruit upon it. This little tree, however, had no figs and it was probably of no more value than a blueberry bush would be in New Hampshire. It was not upon anyone's land; it was growing wild by the roadside. There are places in New England where a tank sprays the roadsides so that all things growing there wither away. This is to clear the roadside of poison ivy or any unwanted thing, and if there were a blueberry bush, it would also die. Have we a right thus to destroy growing things? I sometimes wonder, but if we can even contemplate the possibility of having a right to do so, surely the Creator had a right to send forth power merely by His word, and cause this thing to wither away.

But why did He do it? It would be hard to believe that it was simply in a moment of irritation, because that would be contrary to His nature. Jesus could get roaringly, gloriously angry at the evils and hypocrisy of mankind, but there is no record of His becoming pettishly irritated at little troubles of His own.

I believe that He desired to show that God can *either create or destroy*. There is a power of God that can enter into created substance and cause it to wither away, and the disciples saw it do so right before their eyes. But then He carried this much further. He stated that this same power could enter into even a mountain and cause it to move, if the person who said to it, "Be thou removed," could believe it.

Is there any reason and any need for us in our day even to consider such nature miracles? We have thought not, but unless we can learn to step forth in faith and to exert this healing power of God, not only upon individuals but upon the earth upon which we live, this very earth is likely to hurl many people to destruction.

Jesus did not strike Pontius Pilate or the Pharisees dead, but He did strike dead a wild fig tree, to show that the power to do such a thing was in His world. However, I do not at the moment imagine us walking the roadside and saying to the poison ivy, "Wither away!" though I sometimes wish that we could do so!

But there is another matter in which I have said, "Wither away!" in the prayer of faith, and have pictured the unwanted growing things withering away exactly as the roots of the fig tree withered away. I have said it to the roots of cancer. A medical doctor great in prayer once gave me these words of wisdom. He said: "When you pray for the healing of cancer it will be more powerful if, instead of just saying, 'Oh Lord, pour out your life upon this person,' you say instead, 'Oh Lord, enter into this person with your red ray, with your destructive energy, and burn out in this person whatever cells are out of order. Let them be destroyed. Let them wither away, as the fig tree withered away from its roots.' And, after you have prayed thus," said the doctor, "then speak the word of power, and advise the body of the person from this time forth to make only adult, normal cells in perfect order and harmony, because the different forms of cancer are actually cells growing wild, multiplying too rapidly after the pattern of childhood."

This has been by no means a cure-all, because as I have intimated more than once, such diseases are not merely diseases of the individual. They are diseases of our civilization, and therefore the healing of them will continue to be difficult, both spiritually and medically, until we see what we are doing in our civilization. As a matter of fact, I have seen very few real and, shall I say, dramatic cures of cancer by prayer, but I have seen an occasional such cure, and the concept of the withering away of the unwanted cells has added power to the prayer.

Of course, you may say, God knows what to do without our telling Him. Yes, of course He does. But our prayers seem to be more powerful if they are expressed in words that more correctly instruct the inner being of the person—the cells of the body perhaps, or the subconscious mind (whatever the subconscious mind may be)—and give it a more exact picture and order of what to do.

At the moment, however, Jesus did not connect this miracle of the fig tree with cancer, a disease not yet known. He connected it, surprisingly enough, with a mountain! "If ye have faith, and doubt not, ye shall not only do this which is done to the fig tree, but also if ye shall say unto this mountain, Be thou removed, and be thou cast into the sea; it shall be done." (Matt. 21:21)

If we can really speak unto a mountain, and command it to move into the midst of the sea, as Jesus said, then surely by that same power we can speak to a mountain and command it to stay fast and not be moved, save for that gentle quivering that settles the tensions within the faults of the earth. This power cannot be proved. But God demands not proof but faith. (In fact, if a spiritual power could be proved it would lose its power, because the power comes from faith.)

I have not had the faith, nor the occasion, to speak to a mountain and tell it to be moved into the midst of the sea. But I have had the occasion and a bit of faith, inspired by the fig tree, to speak to a mountain and suggest that it stay quietly where it is, settling its tensions in a gentle manner. Most of you who read this probably respond immediately with disbelief, because you have not had the occasion to consider the power of prayer over mountains and the fault of the earth beneath them. Probably your earth stays firm beneath your feet. But if you lived where from time to time you can feel it quiver, or even rock like a boat on the high sea, you would instinctively pray for protection. In fact, such prayer is included in the Episcopal Prayer Book. And I am assured that such prayer has power.

It is very strange that most people feel that they cannot pray for the healing of the earth. The most righteous ones will say, "But it is prophesied . . ." and speak gloatingly of the great tribulation, which seems to afford them joy and contentment, I do not know why. Of course they, being the elect, expect to be caught up in the air to be with Jesus and to escape the tribulation. That is all very well, but do they have no children—no friends—no little ones upon the earth for whom to care?

This may be one of the last stands of the great apostasy, which is that the hand of God is shortened so that He cannot save, and that all the terrible things that happen are His will and must be accepted. Yet it is also prophesied that there will be plagues of illness, and do we therefore refrain from trying to help the sick? Do we refuse doctors because the Bible says that in the latter days there shall be great plagues? (Rev. 9:6; 11:6; 15:1; 18:8; 21:9)

Real prophecy always contains an "if," If there had been so many as ten righteous people through whom God could have worked, Sodom and Gomorrah would not have been destroyed. (Gen. 18:23ff.)

I remember the first time I came to understand that God is greater than fate. A lady called me in great grief, because her husband was dying in a hospital in Philadelphia. She had been to a fortune-teller six weeks previously and had been told that in six weeks her husband would die. So—what was I to say? I asked the Lord and He put in my mouth the words, "God is greater than fate. Even if according to natural laws your husband would have died in six weeks, even if that is the way fate stacked the cards, God can reshuffle the deck."

We prayed, claiming God's power to change the laws of probability that we call fate, and He changed them. Her husband recovered.

Jesus had power over the fig tree, a power to create or to destroy. He still has power over the earth whence the fig tree grew, power enough even to reverse the natural laws of cause and effect, whose outworking we call "fate." And I know furthermore that He exerts this power through those who are willing to pray the prayer of faith for the healing of the earth.

Perhaps you are thinking, "Oh, I just can't believe that!" Well then, don't! But if your house ever catches on fire, and you hear the flames roaring up to heaven, and you feel the fierce wind driving those flames further, you might like to pray that a spiritual power will speak to the wind, and that the wind will die down. This can happen. I know, for I have tried it. Or if it is not dangerous to other houses, you might pray for the wind to change, as of that moment, and blow strongly from the opposite direction, and this also can happen. My sister-in-law did this one time. "Lady, run!" said a passerby, driving up a steep canyon road. "You'll be burned to a crisp."

"No, I won't!" said she, and continued to pray and to hose the roof of her house. At that moment the wind changed and blew toward the mountains where there were no houses, and soon the fire was controlled.

How intelligent would she have been if she had said, "But the Bible says that there will be much destruction and tribulation in the latter days," and refrained from praying and from spraying the roof?

If you are ever in a storm in a small boat, you might try praying for protection and then saying, as Jesus did to the wind and the waves, "Peace, be still!" (Mark 4:39) And if you do not doubt in your heart, if you believe it from the depths of your consciousness, it is entirely possible that you will see the result. How many people were praying at Dunkirk? No one knows. But I know myself that waters can be stilled, and that the wind can abate its energy because of prayer. I have tried it, and it has happened.

Some people cannot pray thus because they do not love the earth. One time after a long drought, when rain had finally come, a woman entered my door and said, "Oh, I'm so glad the sun came out again. I prayed all the way for the sun to shine, so I'd have a happy trip." She did not care about the earth. She did not even *see* the earth, nor feel any kinship with it. And so it was nothing for her to pray gaily for sunshine, when the parched earth needed rain.

Kinship with the earth is partly love and concern for the earth, but it goes deeper than that. As we abide in Christ, there comes to many of us a sense of being *part* of the earth. We feel within us the moving of power, so that we can speak forth the word and know that through that word an actual energy is entering into the earth, or the wind, or the clouds, or water, so that it will obey God through us.

Some will not believe this, but others of you will find your hearts lifted up, and you will think, "Oh, I have always hoped that this could be true, but no one has ever said it!" It is for you who hope that I am writing. It is to you that I say: trust the feeling of your own heart! Dare to trust. If a burden is laid upon you, if you feel within you a sadness that you cannot explain, an ominous feeling, a sense of dread for unknown reasons, say to the Lord, "What is it?" Perhaps He will tell you that there is danger in such an area. Then pray! Even though you do not know what the threat may be, you can say, "Lord, let your spiritual power go forth to avert or mitigate whatever danger is coming upon the land."

So do not be afraid if you have the gift of prophecy, feeling beforehand the coming of danger or trouble. That gift is given to you so that you can pray. You can never prove the results of your prayer. Nor do I say that all danger and trouble can be averted.

Nevertheless, pray in faith and give thanks to our Lord Jesus, not only for the simple miracles, the easily understood ones, of healing and salvation. Give thanks also for the strange and mysterious, the borderline, the fringe miracles, such as the two considered in this chapter, because they show the deep truth that underlies all miracles: the complete connection between nature and life and God.

12
A Chapter of Healings

"The Bible is the story of the relationship between God and man and the earth. The hero or protagonist of the Bible is God. God is a Spirit, infinite, eternal, and unchangeable, in His being, wisdom, power, holiness, justice, goodness and truth." *(Westminster Shorter Catechism)* An infinite Spirit is more than a spiritual body, nor can we conceive of God in any kind of body, either physical or spiritual. Nevertheless, we say not only that He is Spirit but that He is a Spirit and we are correct. For his ever-prevading Spirit permeated by His divine mind can reason and think and feel and control and order. He is, in other words, supernatural. And the attempt of rationalism to press Him within the mold of our human minds has resulted indeed in death, but not to Him! "He that sitteth in the heavens shall laugh: the Lord shall have them in derision." (Ps. 2:4) The death of dry-rot is coming, rather, to those churches that demote their Creator from His throne and endeavor to be merely ethical groups concerned with social service.

The Gospels in almost every verse proclaim the supernatural power of God through Jesus Christ. We are wise if we at least consider the possibilities that their accounts of His miracles may be true, for if we do not, we so emasculate and cripple the Bible that its healing and saving power is utterly destroyed.

A minister who is also a psychologist lectured at a school of pastoral care on the supernatural aspect of the Bible. His secretary had cut out of an old Bible all verses dealing with the supernatural: miracles, visions (sleeping and awake), angels, demons, and so forth. He had these discarded passages put in a plastic bag, and during the lecture he held up the bag and the denuded Bible before us. There was more of the Bible in the bag than between the covers of the book!

Therefore, let us now consider the healing miracles of Jesus with an open mind, taking Matthew 8 as our outline.

"And, behold, there came a leper and worshipped him, saying, Lord, if thou wilt, thou canst make me clean. And Jesus put forth his hand, and touched him, saying, I will; be thou clean. And immediately his leprosy was cleansed. And Jesus saith unto him, See thou tell no man; but go thy way, show thyself to the priest, and offer the gift that Moses commanded, for a testimony unto them." (Matt. 8:2-4)

Jesus put forth His hand and touched him, although leprosy was a most disgusting illness, and furthermore was considered to be highly contagious. Why did He touch him? He touched him because He Himself was a living channel of the power of God. The original light of the Creator filled Him so much that it went forth through Him and from Him. It could shine out of His Spirit like the light of electricity. It could also move through His body like the heat of a hot iron, or an electric stove. When He made a physical contact with the other person there was a double channel for the power, which could therefore work far more effectively. So touching the leper He prayed the prayer of faith, or in the words of the Bible He sent forth the word of power: "Be thou clean!"

What is the prayer of faith? We read in James 5:15, "The prayer of faith shall save the sick, and the Lord shall raise him up." Apparently the prayer of faith makes a channel between God and the sick person, so that the Lord can raise him up. This prayer is quite simply just what it says: a prayer of faith, not a prayer of worship or a prayer of contemplation, valuable though they are. Nor is it a prayer of vain repetition, of beseeching, though that too has its place. (E.g., Luke 18:1-8) The prayer of faith calmly and quietly asks for a specific thing and then sends forth the word of power, either saying, "Let it be so," which is the literal translation of the word "Amen," or saying in more simple words, as I am apt to do: "Thank you, Lord. I believe that your power is entering into this person, working toward the wholeness that I see in my mind. Amen."

For further discussion of the prayer of faith I have already suggested *The Healing Light.* Or if one desires a deeper study of this matter in the form of parables, one might read my teaching novels. The first, *Oh, Watchman,* is case history on case history, put in the form of a story, of the prayer of faith going forth even to people who did not believe, even to the ignorant, even to Jewish people who did not accept Christ. While the story is contrived, every one of the incidents of healing in that book is true, and the manner of performing them is told as definitely and carefully and simply. as I know how to tell it. In reading that book, you will also see, among other truths, the reason and the value for touching the sick person if in any way possible. One then become a connected channel, and therefore the power is transferred more readily, more quickly, and far, far more effectively. Many prayer groups begin with great enthusiasm and end with staleness, boredom, and disillusionment. And if they ask me the reason, I say, "Do you go to see people, and pray for them with the laying on of hands?"

They are apt to reply, "Oh, no!" sounding shocked and astonished, although just in the breath before that they have told me that *The Healing Light* is their "Bible"; they kept it on the bedside table.

There is value in prayer from a distance, of course. We do this in church continually, and various groups interested in the study of prayer have learned how to focus this power and make it more effective. I know of many miracles done through the power of intercession:

that is, of prayer from a distance. But I know other healings that might have been accomplished had there been a direct contact but that did not take place merely through the prayers of a prayer group. In fact, I have been told by prayer-group members, "Nothing seems to work." Why? I am sure that the multitude would not have been healed if Jesus had merely called together His disciples and had a prayer group about them. People came to Him, or He went to them, and He touched them and healed them individually. It was a much more sacrificial way, but it was the way that He usually followed. I can only say to prayer-group members: "Go forth and do this work as Jesus did." If one does not make the effort of going to the person and being in direct contact with him, after a while one's power is apt to fail and one's interest to flag.

Jesus said to the leper who was healed, "Tell no man." (Matt. 8:4) He often gave that warning to those whom He had healed. Some people conclude from this that He did not want people to know Him as a miracle-worker. I do not believe this. When John the Baptist sent messengers to Him to say, "Art thou He that should come? or shall we look for another?" (Luke 7:20), Jesus answered, "Go your way, and tell John what things ye have seen and heard; how that the blind see, the lame walk, the lepers are cleansed, the deaf hear, the dead are raised, to the poor the gospel is preached." (Luke 7:22)

I believe that He said, "Tell no man," in order to protect the one who was healed. I have found out by grim experience that to arise and testify too soon concerning a healing is apt to bring back the trouble. Why? First of all, the spirit within a person is shy. The growing edge of the soul is very sensitive. Therefore, telling another person of a healing is apt to disturb this brooding inner spirit of man. Second, when one rises and testifies one is apt to be met by cynicism. People look at the person and think, "I wonder how long that will last." The subconscious mind of the person picks up this feeling of uncertainty, and therefore faith is apt to be weakened.

However, Jesus further instructed this man: "But go thy way, show thyself to the priest, and offer the gift that Moses commanded, for a testimony unto them." (Matt. 8:4) Jesus would hardly have been vitally interested concerning the priest's receiving a pair of turtle-doves or two young pigeons. Why then did He tell him to give a thank-offering to the priest? He told him that because, just as idle chatter or even genuine testifying is apt to frighten the spirit, so an act of faith, such as the giving of a thank-offering, is apt to console and strengthen the spirit. The inner being requires it. If we really feel that a healing power has entered into us, then why would we not desire to give a thank-offering?

If one is healed by God through the prayers of an individual, there is nothing wrong in the hearty desire to give a gift of gratitude to that individual. Furthermore, there is nothing wrong in that individual accepting it. Many of those who do healing work stand in the light of those for whom they pray because in a form of pride, or embarrassment, they do not like to accept such gifts. One needs to learn gracious acceptance just as one needs to learn gracious giving.

If the person who does the healing is being paid a salary for his spiritual work—that is, if he is a minister —then it would be appropriate though not necessary for him to give this gift to his church. If, however, the person who does the healing work has no salary at all, then it would be better for him to use the gift in order to keep alive the life that is in him. No matter how "spiritual" a person is, he or she is still under the necessity of eating! Jesus Himself and His followers apparently accepted the thank-offerings of the people. They carried the bag (John 12:6) in which their money was kept. Not one of them went out to work in order to earn this money; it was given to them, naturally. When Jesus sent His disciples out two by two, He told them they need not take any extra thing with them, no extra coat or food or money. (Mark 6:8-9)

Everything they needed would be provided. How? By God dropping it from heaven? Hardly! It would more likely be provided in the most spontaneous and natural and helpful way, by the gifts of those who were healed.

The next story of healing in Matthew, Chapter 8, concerns a Roman captain. He came to Jesus, saying, "Lord, my servant lieth at home sick of the palsy, grievously tormented." (Matt. 8:6) A servant in those days was what we would call a slave. The system of employing people to work in a home had not yet come into being. We deplore slavery. Nevertheless it is comforting to realize that in many cases even if a servant was not paid a salary, he was loved and cherished as long as he lived. In those days there was no need of the government providing social security. Anyone who had someone working for him assumed the responsibility of taking care of him.

Here was a centurion with a servant who was utterly useless. He was sick of the palsy, a type of paralysis. Nevertheless, the centurion loved and cherished him, and even went so far as to go to this wandering Jewish prophet and to "lose face," as one might say, by asking Him to heal the man. "And Jesus saith unto him, I will come and heal him. The centurion answered and said, Lord, I am not worthy that thou shouldest come under my roof: but speak the word only, and my servant shall be healed." (Matt. 8:7-8) This is intensely interesting. It is true that Jewish society considered it unworthy for a Jew to come under the roof of a Gentile. Such was the social order of the day, and the centurion adhered to it.

Jesus did not say, "Oh, but I shall insist upon coming under your roof." This would have been "social action," which did not interest Him at all. He was interested, rather, in the centurion's statement of faith. (Matt. 8:8-9) He said to them that followed, "Verily I say unto you, I have not found so great faith, no, not in Israel." (Matt. 8:10)

"And Jesus said unto the centurion, Go thy way; and as thou hast believed, so be it done unto thee. And his servant was healed in the selfsame hour." (Matt. 8:13) This is an example of a healing through intercession, through prayers from a distance which, as I have said, Jesus very seldom did. It was made possible by the centurion's great and wide-open channel of self-sacrificial faith.

I have said that Jesus never made a demonstration for the purpose of changing or reforming the social order of His day. Search the Scriptures and you will see that it is so! That is why they crucified Him. They expected that when the Messiah would come, He would rally the people around Him, start a revolution, form a new social order, and set the country free from the Roman Empire. He did not do those things at all. Why? Didn't He care? Did He not desire to see slavery abolished, and the status of women raised, and people free to worship God as they pleased? Of course He desired these things, but He was doing the greater thing. He was preparing the power that eventually would bring this to pass, and that was the power of the Holy Spirit. Later on, when the Holy Spirit had come, and therefore sufficient power was available, He directed Peter to do the very thing that He did not do: to go to the house of a Gentile centurion and pray for him and his friends. (Acts 10:1ff.)

People of today busy themselves with the minor matters of social reform, without first seeking and acquiring the power of the love of God through the Holy Spirit that alone will make this great work successful. They mean well, but they are like people continually making new electric contrivances without having the current of electricity to run them. One might imagine them saying, "Oh, isn't that too bad! I was sure *this* would work, and look, it's not working. Let's go and try again. Let's make another type of electric heater, or electric stove." But unless they are connected with electricity, it does not matter what type of gadget they make. Their contrivances are only cast upon the dump at last; their committees die; their projects fail, because the power that alone can make them work is insufficient.

Now let us continue with the stories in this chapter of Matthew.

"And when Jesus was come into Peter's house, he saw his wife's mother laid, and sick of a fever. And he touched her hand, and the fever left her: and she rose and ministered unto them." (Matt. 8:14-15) Luke 4:39 adds that Jesus "rebuked the fever; and it left her."

He rebuked the germ that was causing the disease. He rebuked perhaps the little mind within the cells of the body that had picked up a wrong order from the world without and had fallen prey to illness. (To my great delight science has now discovered that there *is* a little mind within the cells of the body that directs the cells as to what they should do. They call it the DNA molecule.) Jesus stood over her (Luke 4:39), He touched her hand (Matt. 8:15), He took her by the hand and lifted her up. (Mark 1:31)

He did not diagnose her either medically or psychologically. It did not matter to Him whether her disease was flu or amoebic dysentery. His Word was sufficient to heal it. It did not matter whether her body was prone to disease because of anger with Peter who was always traipsing around after Jesus instead of staying at home with his wife, or whether it was caused by feelings of rejection from early childhood. His Word was sufficient to heal her, both soul and body. There are times, true, when we need the diagnosis of a doctor or the analysis of a psychiatrist. But so long as we limit ourselves to these and are content with them, feeling that everything can be healed either by medicine or counseling, we are not doing the works of Jesus. We are doing what we can on a physical and psychological level, but we are not striding the earth as the sons of God, rebuking every deviation from His will and re-establishing by the word of power the wholeness of His creation.

Indeed, we are sometimes so far away from this

"divine madness" that we encourage the devil by saying that illness is the will of God. We might as well say that plant lice and fungi are the will of the gardener, or that a house so poorly built that it cannot stand up straight is the will of the contractor.

Jesus never questioned whether or why He should heal. Nor did anyone ever say to Him, "Why do you make men whole?" The reason was obvious: because God made men in His image and likeness and they were *supposed* to be whole.

But is not illness sometimes a punishment for sin? Does it not stem at times from an unworthy state of mind? Sometimes, yes. In Old Testament days it may always have been in the nature of punishment for the sin of the sick person. But as the centuries passed, sin spread like a miasma through the race and through the genes of the race, and lurked in the very air and in the ground that still laments the shedding of our brother's blood. And the unworthy state of mind of the sick person may be due to his own sin, but may also be the unbearable weight and burden of the sins of the world. Nevertheless, the Word of our Lord spoken by faith is able to forgive that sin, and lift that burden, and heal the disease.

Following the above incident, a multitude came to Jesus and He healed them all. (Matt. 8:16) He did not heal all the sick people of the land, but all who came to Him with the faith to be healed, or, like the centurion, with faith for the healing of one unable to come. Can we step forth and do so great a work as this? Well, no, not very likely. We are not as yet endued with so much power. But we shall receive power after the Holy Ghost is come upon us. (Acts 1:8)

He has indeed come (Acts 2), and the power awaits our finding and using it.

There follow in Matthew 8 two brief conversations so over-condensed that they are hard to understand. If you are looking through this chapter with me you may encounter them and think, "I wonder what Jesus meant by that?" So let me tell you what I think He meant by two of the things He said. It is very simple, really. He said, to one who wanted to follow Him, "The Son of man hath not where to lay his head." This is often taken to indicate extreme poverty. But Jesus' father was God and He was heir to all the riches of the universe, nor is there anything in the Bible to indicate that He lacked for money. I think He was simply showing this man in dramatic fashion that to follow Him would of necessity mean to be a wanderer with no settled abiding-place. He did not want the man to dart off after Him on an impulse without fully understanding the sacrifice it would entail.

Similarly with the other overenthusiastic follower. I can understand this conversation the better because of my Chinese upbringing. In any reputable family it was the duty of the older son to stay with his father and take care of the complicated proceedings of his death and burial. I do not envision the father lying dead and the son saying, "Let me hurry back and bury him." In an Oriental country if the father were awaiting burial, the son would not be cantering around listening to a traveling evangelist. He probably meant, "My father is old and sick. Let me go and stay with him as long as he needs me, and then I will come and follow you."

And Jesus said, "Let the dead bury their dead." (Matt. 8:22) In other words, let those who are dead to spiritual realities attend to earthy matters. There might be a younger son only too glad to succeed to the family responsibility, and probably to a large slice of the family money as well.

Now we come to the story of two madmen and a lot of pigs, and quite appropriately the story begins with a storm. "And when he entered into a ship, his disciples followed him. And, behold, there arose a great tempest in the sea, insomuch that the ship was covered with the waves: but he was asleep. And his disciples came to him, and awoke him, saying, Lord, save us: we perish. And he saith unto them, Why are ye fearful, O ye of little faith? Then he arose, and rebuked the winds and the sea; and there was a great calm. But the men marvelled, saying, What manner of man is this, that even the winds and the sea obey him!" (Matt. 8:23-27)

Jesus of course had control over the wind and the waves. Naturally! But the interesting thing is that He expected His disciples also to have control over the wind and the waves. "O ye of little faith," He really said to them, "why didn't you attend to it and let me finish my nap?"

Is such power as that available to us today? Yes, of course it is, as I know from countless incidents both in my own prayer life and in that of my friends. Why then do we not use it more often? The first reason is that it requires a greater measure of understanding of the earth and the winds and the clouds than most of us possess. Several years ago prayer groups up and down the east coast of the United States prayed that hurricanes would go out to sea so that they would not be troubled by these vast and stormy winds. Whether as the result of prayer, or whether by coincidence, the hurricanes practically ceased. For two or three years there were very few of these storms in the area, and consequently very little rain, and there came a dangerous drought. Then these people of great faith and prayer began to realize that their prayer was misdirected. They learned that God tends the land, and waters it according to His laws of wind and wave, and that therefore they should be cautious in praying the prayer of faith concerning hurricanes. So they changed the manner of their prayer, praying instead that people and property would be spared from damage by the storms which would naturally come.

But the other and greater reason why so few people have any success in praying for the control of winds and clouds, for protection from storms and tempests, fire and earthquake, is simply because they do not have the faith to do so. Nevertheless, if we want this little planet to continue to roll around the sun, and to give us summer and winter, heat and cold, rain and sunshine, we had better pray for greater faith. For we are faced with dangers greater than we know. The sin and violence of the earth and of people upon the earth can so torment the whole planet that it can, as it were, shrug its shoulders and cast man off. And there are plenty of prophecies in the Bible that intimate that this may happen.

To return to this dramatic twenty-four hours in the life of our Lord: "And when he was come to the other side, into the country of the Gergesenes, there met him two possessed with devils, coming out of the tombs, exceeding fierce, so that no man might pass by that way." (Matt. 8:28) The tombs were caves and these two wild men could not in any way be absorbed into society and so there they lived, possessed, as Matthew said, with devils.

The devils knew Jesus. Here is an amazing thing! People who walked the earth, with their minds shrouded in the flesh, did not know that Jesus Christ was the Son of God. Even His disciples at that time were still saying, "What manner of man is this, that even the winds and the sea obey him!" (Matt. 8:27) But these demonic creatures that lived in the bodies of two men knew Jesus, and they said, "What have we to do with thee, Jesus, thou Son of God? art thou come hither to torment us before the time?" (Matt. 8:29)

We may as well face this frightening fact: there are upon this globe living entities who are not human. Some of these are called angels, spiritual beings who are not, and have never been, flesh and blood. They live in the light and the glory of God. They obey Him and do His work, and are often called His messengers. The other kind of nonhuman entities are called devils, or demons. Sometimes they are spoken of as the devil's angels or messengers or servants. The whole Bible from first to last teaches that there is a devil, an enemy, and other evil spirits who work under him.

We took note of this in the third chapter of Genesis. There really is a tempter. There is an adversary. There is an evil being who disobeyed God, and who continually disobeys God, whose will is contrary to the will of God. Whether God intended in the first place that there should be this adversary, that I do not know. This great question of good and evil, the struggle, the back-and-forth rhythm between darkness and light, is one that I do not understand. I only know that it is part of the birthpangs of this earth and of the kingdom of heaven, part of the travail that brings forth life and that is intended to bring forth the sons of God.

We are plainly told here by Matthew, who was a conservative, convention Hebrew, that these men were possessed by devils, and that the devils, being suprahuman or subhuman, therefore had an awareness of the supernatural world and so knew Jesus for what He was.

One of our greatest mistakes is the assumption that everything that is not human is of God. Sirhan Sirhan heard a voice in the summer of 1968 telling him to kill Robert Kennedy, and assumed that the voice was of God. I have no doubt that he heard a voice, and if he accepted the growing doubt even among Christians that there really is a devil, of course he thought that supernatural voice was of God. This does not excuse his action, as anyone should know that God does not tell us to break His own laws. But he would have been more likely to consider this if he had been aware of the fact that God is not the only supernatural being: there is also the devil. (Isa. 14:12, etc.) C.S. Lewis's *The Screwtape Letters* is a brilliant contemporary study of the devil and his methods.

St. Matthew apparently knew more about the hidden causes of mental disturbance than do many modern psychiatrists. He knew that there are subhuman entities, and that they had entered into these two wild men and possessed them: in other words that the root cause of their insanity was possession. I once said to an English psychiatrist of high repute, "Do you believe in the possibility of demon-possession?" And he answered, "Yes, I do. I believe that many patients in our hospitals can be diagnosed as manic-depressive or schizophrenic and these may be true diagnoses, but these troubles on the upper level of the personality may be caused by the infiltration of an evil entity into the lower level of the personality. If this evil entity can be cast out, then it will be much easier to heal the disturbance on the upper level of the personality."

Time without number I have sent forth the word of power and in the name of Jesus Christ commanded an evil spirit to leave a person, and it has departed. I have not written much on this subject for good and sufficient reasons. My only book which contains a case history of exorcism is the autobiographical novel *The Second Mrs. Wu*.

"And there was a good way off from them an herd of many swine feeding. So the devils besought him, saying, If you cast us out, suffer us to go away into the herd of swine. And he said unto them, Go. And when they were come out, they went into the herd of swine: and behold, the whole herd of swine ran violently down a steep place into the sea, and perished in the waters." (Matt. 8:30-32)

There are many other exorcisms recorded in the Bible, but none with such a dramatic outward result as this. Nevertheless I believe it! Sometimes on saying a prayer of exorcism one has to struggle with the indwelling creatures who do not want to leave. When I undertake such spiritual battle, I command them to go not into swine but into the hands of Jesus Christ. I do not tell them to go to hell, for I cannot take this responsibility. But if they are just left to float around in the air, as it were, there is a possibility that they could return and attack this person again, or that they could enter into someone else nearby. My Father, of whom I wrote in *The Second Mrs. Wu,* made quite a study of this entire matter of exorcism, and wrote a book about it called *Demonism Verified and Analyzed*.* One matter perplexed him, however. He said he did not understand why, when a demon was cast out, sometimes

---

*By Hugh White. Obtainable from University Microfilms, Ann Arbor, Michigan.

another person in the family picked up the disturbing spirit. I think that he did not know that the demon had to go somewhere. My father had no herd of swine handy, one might say.

But why did Jesus do this fantastic thing? On other occasions He simply dismissed demons and they departed. Where they went we do not know. Why, therefore, did He allow these demons to enter into the herd of swine who afterward were drowned, being terrified by a disturbing influence that they could not understand? Why?

Many people, of course, become sympathetic about the owner of the swine, just as some people today might become sympathetic toward a doctor or a psychiatrist who lost a fee because his patient was healed by prayer. I do not really concern myself about the swineherd. As a matter of fact, it was doubtless illegal for a Jew to raise swine anyway, since they were considered unclean animals, unfit for food.

Be this as it may, I am sure that Jesus was able to compensate the farmer for the loss of his swine. I don't imagine Him putting His hand into His girdle and saying, "Look, friend, I want to reimburse you for those pigs." But I do imagine Him invisibly blessing that farmer's land, so that the swineherd gained far more than he lost in the swine that ran down into the sea. (Incidentally, the number of the swine seems to increase from Gospel to Gospel as the dramatic story is told. I have known stories thus to increase in present-day life!)

So let us not distract our attention from the main point of this story by worrying about the owner of the pigs. The question remains, however, why did Jesus permit the demons to go into the swine? Maybe He did it to show that demon-possession can be real. Many people would simply say that such an afflicted person is mentally ill, and nothing else. In fact, I would have said so myself some years ago. Sometimes, of course, the person *is* mentally ill. In doing a prayer of exorcism, the most important thing of all is to decide whether it is necessary to make this far-reaching prayer into the worlds of the unknown. One of the worst mistakes that overzealous Christians can make is to run from person to person and cast the devil lightly out of everybody. To assume that anger is demon-possession, fear is demon-possession, mental depression is demon-possession, sin and alcoholism are all demon-possession is a great mistake. I think that C. G. Jung explains the matter thus: a person can unconsciously build in himself a little house of, let us say, hate. In other words, this person can have a personal problem of hate, which can be caused from his own indulgence in feeling and expressing hate. Then it is possible for an entity from without, a thought-form of hate, to come in and live in that house.

Most people, however, are not by any means "possessed." No demon has come to live in their deep unconscious. They themselves have problems, that is all: problems of unforgiveness, or of unhealed fears, or guilt complexes concerning unrepented sin. For someone to rush up to them and say, "Let me cast the devil out of you," would be merely to push the problem deeper into the unconscious. These people do not need exorcism. They need to be honest with themselves, to face their problems, and to work them out with God's help.

However, there are other cases in which the house has been built, and an entity from outside actually has come and taken up residence within that house. This entity may be, as in the case of these two wild men, really and truly one or more demons. Or it may be a gentler thing, some emanation, it would seem, of the soul of a departed person who is lost and who wants to find life within a living person. One should not cast out an evil spirit rudely or unkindly and tell it to go to hell, because one does not know what the nature of this being may be. However, one can never make a mistake by saying, with firmness but with all compassion, "I put you in the hands of Jesus Christ."

Perhaps the reader is thinking: "If there is any truth

to this at all, then isn't this kind of prayer dangerous?" Yes, it certainly is. To get through life without danger is a promise never made to a Christian. And as a matter of fact such a life would be very dull! Yes, it is dangerous. Therefore, one should never embark on a prayer of exorcism unless one is in love and charity with one's fellow men, in union with God, and surrounded with God's protection. Remember the story of the seven sons of Sceva! They undertook to exorcise a possessed man, and he leapt upon them and tore at them and said, "Jesus I know, and Paul I know; but who are ye?" (Acts 19:15)

After casting out a demon, I pray that the love of Jesus will come in and fill up all the empty places where it used to be. And finally I pray that this person will be surrounded with the protection of God, so that nothing can come near to hurt him again.

In all of the years that I have prayed this prayer, I have never known the troubling demon or thought-form to return to the one who has been healed. I have occasionally known what might be called another kind of devil to enter, and the reason for that is that there is still a door open. There is an area in the person's memories that is not healed. There is a relationship in his life that has not been made right. There is a sin in which he is still indulging. Therefore there is a crack in his armor, an open door. But even that crack can be mended, and that door can be closed, and we can really and truly abide in the secret place of the Most High and under the shadow of the Almighty. (Ps. 91:1)

13
Fish and Bread

The story related in John 6:1-14 is told in all four Gospels, and it is told as a sober account of an actual fact. Yet it is a story that very few Christian people believe. I have only twice heard a minister preach upon this subject. One preached upon the generosity of the little boy, that he was willing to share his lunch. The other preached upon the tidy nature of Jesus, who did not want any scraps left around, and ordered the disciples to clean up the place and leave no litter—so the first antilitter law was written in the Gospels!

But to preach upon the subject itself: namely, the great miracle that Jesus did in feeding some five thousand people out of five barley loaves and two small fishes—well, really! The subject is too hot to handle! I say "some five thousand" people. Two of the Gospels record the number as four thousand. Whether this was a different and separate miracle, or whether it was the same one, and the census-taker was off a little bit, that I do not know and it is not important to me. The important thing is: Did this thing happen, or did it not happen?

I want to go over the story from the Gospel of John, although his account of it is rather condensed, and I shall insert some details from the other Gospels. John's account is brief; it is telegraphic; it is not written in a high-flown literary style, and I think the reason is that he was jotting down a sort of outline of something that the other Gospels had already told. John very seldom repeated a miracle told in the other Gospels. Then why did he repeat this particular miracle? If you read St.

180

John 6 you will see why. He was the only one who had the audacity, or the wisdom, or both, to write down for us not only the miracle but also its spiritual meaning, and the comments of our Lord Himself upon it.

Let us read with an open mind, and see whether we can believe and understand it. "And a great multitude followed him, because they saw his miracles which he did on them that were diseased. And Jesus went up into a mountain, and there he sat with his disciples. . . . When Jesus then lifted up his eyes and saw a great company come unto him, he saith unto Philip, Whence shall we buy bread, that these may eat? And this he said to prove him: for he himself knew what he would do." (John 6:2-6)

I wonder how long He had known it. I wonder whether He purposely permitted the multitude to follow Him three days, knowing that they would become exhausted and faint from lack of food.

"Philip answered him, Two hundred pennyworth of bread is not sufficient for them, that every one of them may take a little. One of his disciples, Andrew, Simon Peter's brother, saith unto him, There is a lad here, which hath five barley loaves, and two small fishes: but what are they among so many? And Jesus said, Make the men sit down. . . . So the men sat down, in number about five thousand." (Note the word "about.")

Then Jesus took the loaves; and He lifted up His eyes to heaven, an act of prayer which I know included the prayer of faith, and He blessed the loaves, and He broke them. (Matt. 14:19) He then gave thanks (John 6:11) presumably that the miraculous power of His blessing had entered into the loaves. And He "distributed to the disciples, and the disciples to them that were set down; and likewise of the fishes as much as they would. When they were filled, he said unto his disciples, Gather up the fragments that remain, that nothing may be lost. Therefore they gathered them together, and filled twelve baskets with the fragments of the five barley loaves, which remained over and above unto them that had eaten. Then those men, when they had seen the miracle that Jesus did, said, This is of a truth that prophet that should come into the world." (John 6:11-14)

Take note of the fact that in doing this miracle Jesus did not create food out of nothing. He expanded the material that God had already created. He knew and used a law of expansion. Those who created atomic energy did not create it out of nothing. They used a material that God had already created: uranium. They found laws through which they split the atom, and expanded matter into energy, increasing a thousandfold, a millionfold.

Jesus knew all these laws before any scientists lived upon the face of the earth. So He took what the disciples already had on hand. Bread includes the very life of the earth: wheat grown from soil, watered by rain, nourished by sunshine. And He took also fishes, a step higher on the ladder of life: living creatures nourished in the sea. He then called upon a spiritual law that we do not know, and used a spiritual power that we cannot grasp, to enter into these things and to expand the atoms within them.

Moreover, He involved His twelve disciples in this miracle. He broke off a chunk of bread and it expanded. As it expanded He gave it to them, and they took it to the multitude, and they in turn broke the bread and passed it from person to person.

What would have happened if any one of these disciples had said, "I will not do this silly thing. How can this possibly be?" I am sure that the miracle would have ceased, just as when Peter lost his faith in the power of God to lighten his body and enable him, by what one might call levitation, to walk on the sea, then he began to sink beneath the waves. (Matt. 14:28-31)

So therefore, here was a miracle in which human beings had a part. Jesus gave to them the very bread of life, and He enabled them by faith to receive this bread of life in a new way, with a new life-energy added to it so that their physical needs were filled. There were even fragments left over which were gathered up that they should not be wasted.

Why did Jesus do this stupendous thing? He did it, first of all, because He was sorry for the people, and He wanted them to be fed and comforted before they went home. (Matt. 15:32) He did it, secondly, I am sure, to demonstrate and show forth the fact that through Him we also have the power to order and change and control material things. We have acknowledged this fact, and we have seized upon it in an amazing fashion through the laws of science, through the powers and energies released by the wisdom of men. God has given us minds that we may use them, and all of the tremendous powers unleashed by science are from Him. We may be frightened of them, and we may wish that scientists did not discover them so rapidly. We sometimes tremble to think of the power that can be released without the wisdom to know how to use it constructively: the terrible power that can be used either for creation or for destruction. Nevertheless, God has created these powers. God has created the mind of man, and in spite of all the dangers attached to it we should rejoice and be thankful for every discovery of modern science.

And yet there are things that so far modern science does not know how to do. So far science has not discovered how to correct the poison in the air, or how to raise crops without using insecticides and fertilizers so strong that they may be dangerous to the body of man. We should pray for the increased wisdom and sensitivity of scientists, that they may find new ways and better ways to increase the value of crops, to take care of traffic, and to manage industrial wastes without danger, without poison. But we cannot wait for this! The poison has already been released. Atomic fallout is already here. No one knows how much of the illness of mankind may be caused by this very thing. I maintain that in order to heal diseases, in order to heal individuals, we should pray for the healing of air and water and earth.

We can imagine the love of God flowing into air and water and earth. We can imagine the comfort of God and the healing of God, in ways known only to Him, providing the spiritual antidote to the poisons and tensions that mankind has released upon the earth. This same kind of prayer can accomplish miracles of protection. We talk so much of miracles of healing. There is as great a need, or even a greater need, of miracles of protection, prayers such as we find in the Episcopal Prayer Book: for deliverance from fire and tempest, from earthquake and flood. We have a right to pray for this protection, and we have the power to pray for it.

At this point, of course, many people are apt to think, "Well, why does God permit these things?" just as we are apt to think, "Why does God permit illness? Why doesn't God heal it all by Himself if He wants it healed?" This is too big a question for me. I do not know why, but I observe only that God has made the world after this pattern. We are made in His image and likeness, and to us is entrusted a power of creation; to us is given dominion. We are to carry on by His power the work of creation that He has started for us. He will do His greater part, but we must also do our part.

Indeed I believe even more than this. I believe that whether or not we know how to pray, the earth itself is sensitive to us, and to a greater or less degree responds. Jeremiah continually told his people that they were making of the pleasant world a desolate wilderness. One cause of God's wrath toward the people was that they had failed to care for the land that He had given them. Indeed the Bible plainly and repeatedly says that the wickedness of the people had in some way hurt the land.

Nature responds to love and is desolated by neglect. I know it in my own garden. I love my flowers, and they love me and bloom for me. People say that I have a green thumb, but it is not a green thumb; it is the love of God within me. There is a book on *The Power of Prayer on Plants* by Franklin Loehr. I have never undertaken this type of experimentation, but I do not doubt at all that the message of the book is true. We can pray for things that grow upon the earth, and they respond. Moreover, we have an effect upon our land whether or not we pray. The earth responds to the love of God through the spirits of men.

But if we mean to control the earth itself—if through us little people a holy order of life, a sound society, a beautiful civilizaton, is to be established on this earth, how can we get the power to do it? Let us go back to the story of the feeding of the five thousand in St. John 6 and see what we can make of it.

Jesus could not at that time give a complete, satisfactory explanation of His power. No one would have understood Him.

Therefore, in the feeding of the five thousand He preached a sermon in action. One might call it a parable. Nevertheless, it is also a true event. (It seems to me very important that those who speak of the miracles of the Bible, and use words like parable, symbol, and even myth, should make it clear that these are true events that really did happen, whatever they teach or symbolize. If I give a doll to my little granddaughter, that is a symbol of my love for her. Nevertheless, I really did give her a doll.)

So I believe and know that Jesus really did bless the bread, that the disciples broke it and they continued to believe, and it continued to expand and it fed the multitude, after which the people followed Him looking for more bread, and the Pharisees taunted Him and said, "Our fathers did eat manna in the desert..." (John 6:31) (The multitude can make it hard today for people who receive the power of the Spirit!)

"Then Jesus said unto them, Verily, verily, I say unto you, Moses gave you not that bread from heaven; but my Father giveth you the true bread from heaven." (John 6:32) Notice the word *"giveth* you the true bread from heaven."

"For the bread of God is he which cometh down from heaven, and giveth life unto the world." (John 6:33) So He spoke of Himself, but they did not understand Him. "Then said they unto Him, Lord evermore give us this bread. And Jesus said unto them, I am the bread of life: he that cometh to me shall never hunger;

and he that believeth on me shall never thirst." (John 6:34-35) "The Jews then murmured at him, because he said, I am the bread which came down from heaven. And they said, Is not this Jesus, the son of Joseph, whose father and mother we know? How is it then that he saith, I came down from heaven? Jesus therefore answered and said unto them, Murmur not among yourselves. No man can come to me, except the Father which hath sent me draw him." (John 6:41-44) In other words, He said, "I know that you cannot all understand or believe this." Indeed, I wonder whether He was speaking for them or for us.

He went on to say: "Every man therefore that hath heard, and hath learned of the Father, cometh unto me ... Verily, verily I say unto you, He that believeth on me hath everlasting life. I am that bread of life. Your fathers did eat manna in the wilderness, and are dead. This is the bread which cometh down from heaven, that a man may eat thereof, and not die." (John 6:45-50)

Notice the present tense; notice the word *cometh*. He not only came down from heaven when he was born of the Virgin Mary, but He cometh. He continues to come. How? In a physical body that can be seen? No, in a spiritual body that cannot be seen. This was difficult for the disciples to understand, and Jesus repeated it again and again, even rather insistently, even, it might seem to us, a bit crudely.

"Verily, verily, I say unto you," He said, "Except ye eat the flesh of the Son of man, and drink his blood, ye have no life in you. Whoso eateth my flesh, and drinketh my blood, hath eternal life; and I will raise him up at the last day. For my flesh is meat indeed, and my blood is drink indeed. He that eateth my flesh, and drinketh my blood, dwelleth in me, and I in him. As the living Father hath sent me, and I live by the Father: so he that eateth me, even he shall live by me." (John 6:53-57)

The disciples murmured at this, and I don't blame them. We would murmur too. We would say, "Well, I just don't dig it," or, "I simply can't take that!" That is exactly what the disciples said. They said, "This is an hard saying; who can hear it?" (John 6:60)

And then Jesus said something that begins to explain a mystery so great that it cannot be completely grasped. He said, "It is the spirit that quickeneth; the flesh profiteth nothing." (John 6:63) In other words, even though He used the words, His *body* given for us, His *body* coming down from heaven, nevertheless He said, "It is the spirit that quickeneth." How does He come to us now? He comes to us in His spiritual body. He does not stand by the seashore and cook breakfast for us. (John 21:4-14) How we wish that He did! And yet He comes to us in another way. He does not prepare food for us, but He can *be* the food of life in us.

He can enter into us in a way that is just as real as the entering in of the bread that the multitude ate. That bread and fish was digested by them, and was used to give them strength for the long walk back to their homes. The spiritual energy of Christ can be digested by us also, becoming part of our spirits and minds and even our bodies, and it can give us strength for our long journey home to the kingdom of heaven upon this earth that is our only hope of salvation. For without this bread from heaven all our striving to make this world better only seems to make it worse in ways that are confusing to us and utterly frustrating.

How then can we enact again this miracle of the loaves and fishes? Why, this miracle is enacted Sunday by Sunday and day by day all over the world! The results of it should be tremendous, both shattering and rebuilding the earth. They have not been so. Why? Because we have not completely understood or believed what we are doing when we come to the Communion Service.

Consider: the priest takes the bread in his hands, and lifts up his eyes unto heaven as Jesus did, and says, "Vouchsafe to bless and sanctify with thy word and Holy Spirit these thy gifts and creatures of bread and wine... that we may be partakers of His most blessed body and blood..." He is asking that a miracle take place at that moment in the bread and wine, and that they be changed by the entering in of a spiritual energy as the water was changed at Cana, as the bread was infused with an expanding life upon the mountaintop. Can this possibly be true? I know that it can. A very sensitive Jewish friend of mine once went to church with me, sitting in the pew and not receiving Communion. I asked him whether the service differed in any way from morning prayer, which he had attended with me before. "At first it was the same," he said, "but when the priest lifted up the bread and the cup before the altar, something new came into it."

"What came into it?" I asked. But he could not explain.

Some have seen a light surrounding the holy vessels. But most of us have seen nothing, and not altogether by our own dimness of sight, for the light is shrouded by the darkness of unbelief in the congregation, so that only the very perceptive can behold it. Whether or not we have seen it, however, some of this energy does enter the bread, and it is charged with an ever-expanding life far more wonderful than the life that caused the loaves to expand in Jesus' hands. For this energy is an ever-increasing power flowing from the spiritual body of Jesus into our spirits, and exploding in us the creative principle from which all worlds are made.

His physical body cannot be eaten by us in the form of flesh, and many of us find the crude words of the Communion Service rather repelling. But His spiritual body actually can be received and absorbed by us. This evanescent life enters into our spirits invisibly and impalpably. But since we are one—spirit, mind, and body forming the unity of the total being—therefore this spiritual energy can expand in us and feed the mind with new inspiration, and the body with new life. This new life can activate and increase within us the natural recuperative powers of the body, and so bring about healing. If we prepare ourselves to receive the power and to carry through this miraculous work, then direct healing can be received through the Communion Service.

We prepare ourselves to receive by house-cleaning, so that the heavenly guest can enter with rejoicing. He is love. He is goodness. Therefore He finds it difficult to make His way into us when we are filled with hate and dirtiness. Hence the service begins with the reading of the Ten Commandments, reminding us that if we want the Holy One to come into us, we must do our best to make ourselves holy. This is the reason for the commandments of God which Jesus Christ re-emphasized and expanded in Matthew, Chapter 5-7. They are the rules for training for the life of the Spirit. When a young man wants to play football, he goes into training. When a person wants to exert power to save his country and his world, it is also necessary to go into training. When we fail to do so—when we minimize or even deny the rightness of His commandments—then we lose our feeling of His reality, and someone comes up with the remark, "God is dead." He is dead in those who say it, that is all. They have killed His life in their own souls. But He is most ferociously alive in the universe. Having created it He can destroy it, as He showed in the miracle of the fig tree, studied in a preceding chapter. And unless we repent and come unto the Lord, and cease from our evil ways, He may show forth that power by a rage of destruction.

Now take note: Jesus broke the bread and passed it to the disciples, and they to the multitude. And we, when we receive this life from Him, are to pass it on to the multitude, to the world. We are to be like lights, like cities set upon a hill so that their light cannot be hid. (Matt. 5:14) It should be possible actually to recognize a Christian by the joy and the power that shine forth through him. When Jesus said, "Let your light so shine before men, that they may see your good works, and glorify your Father which is in heaven" (Matt. 5:16), I do not think that He was referring to the passing of the collection plate in church. Can you imagine someone saying, "Oh, praise God! He put a dollar into the plate"? But you can imagine someone saying, "Oh, praise God! This man prayed for me and I was healed!"

The Communion Service is not the only channel for receiving the life of God, but it is a very profound channel, involving symbolism that speaks not only to the conscious mind but also to the unconscious. The ancient and rather brutal words in which some of this eternal mystery is expressed are quite comprehensible to the remnant of the old inherited mind within us.

However, some people prefer to receive this power of the Spirit in more ethereal ways, simply by the lifting up of the consciousness into His kingdom so that His power may enter into our spirits. This is the way of the Society of Friends. It is also the way of many contemplative groups and societies, and this way I use myself every morning. Before trying to tackle the day's work, I repair to my study (with a cup of coffee) and for an hour keep my mind open to the entering in of His spiritual body: the bread of life. For I need every channel that I can find. I need to apprehend Him in the relayed fashion, by the channeling of His power through the bread and wine at the altar, and I also need to tune my mind to His mind every morning, that through the day I may walk in His power and in His light.

When I thus feed on His bread of life, as the multitude did upon the mountaintop, everything within me comes to life. I can look upon the work of that day and feel within me the power and the wisdom to do it. And I can look even upon the problems and dangers of the world around me and not be dismayed, knowing that greater than the power of evil in this world is the power of life through Jesus Christ, and through us little ones who act as His channels.

14
They Dropped Dead

✳

Sorry, but they did drop dead, as Uzzah dropped
dead when he touched the ark of the covenant. (2 Sam.
6:7) Ananias and his wife Sapphira thought up a little
scheme for short-changing the church, just as people
today...finish the sentence for yourselves. They sold a
piece of land and came and gave the price to the church,
laying it at Peter's feet. But it was not the whole price,
although they said it was. When Peter challenged first
the one and then the other with this dishonesty, each
one had a heart attack, or a stroke or something, and
died. (Acts 5:1-11)

Why? Was this the result of that entering in of the
body of Christ described in the preceding chapter? In
a way, yes. The power of God is still a dangerous power.
The little group that was the first church had received
this power in a body, after praying together for ten
days. It rushed in from heaven with such force that one
could feel it in the air like a wind, one could see it
shining like tongues of fire on the heads of those who
were filled with it, and one could perceive the immediate signs of its working in the spirit, mind, and body.

One of these signs was that they spoke in languages
that they did not know: real languages understood by
those who heard them. (Acts. 2:1-13) Much has been
written about this in many books, including my own
The Healing Gifts of the Spirit and, in more scholarly
fashion, Morton Kelsey's book *Tongue Speaking*. It is
simply the bringing to life of one of the many unused
abilities of the unconscious mind. This "other one of

us" lives beyond time and space, and therefore is able to hear any language spoken anywhere at any time. The lips speak then not at the impulse of the conscious mind but at the impulse of the unconscious: the spirit-mind.

Nevertheless I do not believe that this speaking in tongues is the only gift of the Spirit, or even that it is necessarily the first gift or sign of the presence of the Spirit. The first sign at Pentecost was the shaking of the air in the room, described as a rushing mighty wind. In Acts 4:31 we read, "And when they had prayed, the place was shaken where they were assembled together; and they were all filled with the Holy Ghost." Last week we held a School of Pastoral Care in the California mountains. When we prayed together at our final meeting, the place was shaken where we were assembled together. And the power of the Holy Ghost was renewed in all of us. It was not an earthquake. The breath of God breathed upon us.

The second sign that was seen at Pentecost was a current of light or fire like "cloven tongues as of fire" that appeared upon the heads of those present. At my own first receiving of the Holy Ghost I felt that fire burning within the head, as did the two who prayed with me. We did not see the double current of energy that came into us, but the burning of it was deep and intense, and accompanied by great joy. And it was, I know, a transformation even of the physical being so that we could better apprehend the Spirit of God.

The third step in the pentecostal invasion of man by God was an awakening and quickening of all the gifts potential to his nature. Nine of these gifts are listed by St. Paul in 1 Corinthians 12, beginning most aptly with the gifts of wisdom and of knowledge. That these gifts were given at Pentecost is evident from the text of Acts 2. For instance, Peter who until this time had been rather a bungling person, now stood up and preached a sermon of such depth and power that three thousand people were converted in one day.

St. Paul goes on to mention gifts of faith, healing, miracles, prophecy and discernment, and as we read on through the books of Acts we see all these gifts operative in the lives of the apostles from this time forth. Finally he mentions tongues, and interpretation, or the ability to grasp and say in one's own language some message received through "praying in the Spirit," as the gift of tongues is often called. (Eph. 6:18) Moreover at the end of the same chapter St. Paul mentions gifts of "helps" and "governments." It seems to me that the Holy Spirit simply explodes in the person those gifts that are part of his original nature. The Holy Spirit makes one a better teacher, a better writer, a better disciplinarian of one's children, a better machinist or inventor or house-cleaner.

What was this transforming power if it was not the spiritual body of Christ that He promised them? And what was that bread from heaven if it was not called in other words the Holy Spirit, the Comforter, the strength-giver? Some of you may understand the theology of all this better than I do.

How can three persons be one person? For I do not pretend to grasp it. It is a mystery. If they—or He— were physical beings, it would be ridiculous. But they —or He—are spiritual in being and in power. The best explanation (or symbolism) concerning this that I have read is in Dorothy Sawyer's book *The Mind of the Maker*. In writing a book, she explains, first of all comes the father-idea: the concept, the plan. Without it there can be no book. Everything comes from this master-concept, and to it everything is referred. Next, the concept must take form. It is written down by a person with hands of flesh. But there is still no use in this unless the book is made available. Therefore, the last goingforth of creativity is the publishing of the book so that it can belong to every person who wants to buy it.

When Jesus went back to heaven, taking with him humanity which He had redeemed, there was a new merger of God and man: the original Holy Spirit who brooded over the waters in the beginning (Gen. 1) somehow entering into the redeemed spirit of mankind so that a spiritual power of God became available—to anyone who would pay the price for it. That price is faith and obedience. The disciples paid that price, but in their enthusiasm they went a little bit overboard and added to the price, as Christians are apt to do, to their discomfort. They were so filled with love that they wanted to live all together, as some people like to do today. In fact, you might say that the early Christians were the first hippie community! They had everything in common. Anyone who owned land sold it, and brought the money to the hippie heaven, and gave it to all. Now Jesus had not required this, and neither had that great exponent of Christianity, St. Paul. True, marriage was not for him. He was too busy being St. Paul. Nevertheless, he expected most people to live in families, as God in the beginning had ordained for them to do, for the purpose of creativity. In Ephesians 5:22-6:9 we find Paul's advice not only to fathers, mothers and children but also to servants, building that great foundation of society, a home.

No doubt the early Christians had a wonderful vision of the power of prayer that could be generated by a group of holy people all living together, separated from the world. In this they were right. There are enclosed and cloistered communities of those who have given up everything and entered a monastery or convent in order to live in continual contemplation and honor God by their prayer and the work of their hands. No one can measure the spiritual benefit of such lives. These people are undertaking the most difficult and most sacrificial way of prayer; they are making reparation for the sins of the world. Surely this is one way of taking up the cross of Christ and following Him. They are endeavoring insofar as possible to live without sin, so that they can better pray for forgiveness for the sins of the world. This, I feel sure, is the underlying purpose of holy communities, even though as the long centuries have passed men may have lost sight of this purpose or doubted its value. I believe that if monks and nuns add to the sacrificial living of their holy community a deeper understanding of the prayer of faith, the course of history would change before them, as before no other power in the world.

However, only certain ones are called to this rigorous celibate life. Most people are supposed simply to "be fruitful and multiply and replenish the earth" (Gen. 1:28), as God commanded Adam in the first place. Little children need their own home and father and mother. This security in family love is their basic need, even greater than that of food and clothing. The early Christians rather forgot children in their plan for community living. But before the change away from the system of community living was made, tragedy came to Ananias and Sapphira, his wife, because they desired the joy and power of the new life, but did not quite want to pay the full price for it.

I have a certain sympathy for these two people! Maybe they felt uneasily that it should not be necessary for Christians to have all things in common, since so far as we know Jesus Christ never commanded or recommended this way of life for all His followers. Ananias and Sapphira were not *required* to sell their field and give the money to the apostles. (Acts 5:4) But this was the "done" thing, and they wanted to be in with the crowd. They were required, however, to tell the truth, to keep the commandment of honesty, and this commandment (Exod. 20:16) they broke. They bore false witness. They let it be believed that the money they brought was the full price for the land. St. Peter knew this by the gift of discernment, and he challenged them. He gave them a chance to confess that it was not the full price, and to ask forgiveness. If they had been willing to do so they would have been forgiven and reinstated in favor with God and man. But in confusion and guilt they missed their opportunity. "You're sure that's what you were paid for the land?" asked Peter. And Sapphira said, "Yes sir, it sure is," or words to that effect.

Thereupon Peter uttered these terrifying words: "How is it that ye have agreed together to tempt the Spirit of the Lord? behold, the feet of them which have buried

thy husband are at the door, and shall carry thee out."
(Acts 5:9)

And Sapphira fell at his feet and died.

Did Peter pray for her to die? I hope not! I hope,
rather, that he knew that she would die, just as he knew
that she was lying. But *why* would she die? People lie
that much all around us and they don't drop dead.
People lie about the price of this and the cost of that,
and about their income taxes, and about customs and
debts and tithes, and they don't drop dead. Or do they?

What really happened to Ananias and Sapphira? My
guess would be something like this: the power of the
Holy Spirit was flowing at a great rate through that
little church, and it came up against another current—
evil and deception—and there was an explosion. There
is an alternating current of electricity and there is a
direct current, and when they come together it causes
an explosion. It is possible to light a lamp with either
current, but not with both at the same time. And the
church was so strongly charged with the power of the
Holy Spirit that the burst of the explosion caused some
kind of shock that proved fatal to these two misguided
people.

We would be very much upset if someone in the
church of today said, "This is my tithe," and if the
minister said, "Why are you trying to trick God?" and
the man fell dead and the ushers had to carry him out.
But the chances of its happening are slight. There is not
that much of a charge of the Holy Spirit in the church
of today.

I am not sure whether that is a good or bad thing.
Nor am I sure that a form of death does not take place,
for this very reason: grieving the Holy Spirit by hypocrisy. A man of the world would not drop dead if discovered in deceit. He would think, "Well, I didn't get
away with it that time," and would promptly figure out
some other trick. Those charged with the Holy Spirit
are in the most danger of sinning against God and being
hurt by it.

The shock to Ananias and Sapphira was, first of all,

to their spirits. It was like a door slamming shut, a door between themselves and God. And it was not God who shut that door; they did. The reverberation of that slam affected mind and body with such force that the heart stopped beating.

Nevertheless, there was a cleansing within the church, and its result was a tremendous new surge of power. "And believers were the more added to the Lord ... insomuch that they brought forth the sick into the streets, and laid them on beds and couches, that at the least the shadow of Peter passing by might overshadow some of them. There came also a multitude ... bringing sick folks ... and they were healed every one." (Acts 5:14-16)

The result therefore of the cleansing of the church was more life, more healing and more power, so much more that even prison doors could not hold the disciples. (Acts 5:19)

There is death in the church today. To some, the church has become merely a political or social organization that considers its main function to be "social action," the one thing that Jesus studiously avoided. Once a man came to Jesus with a perfectly sensible grievance and said, "Speak to my brother, that he divide the inheritance with me. And he said unto him, Man, who made me a judge or a divider over you?" (Luke 12:13-14) He could easily have undertaken that bit of social action. He could have investigated the matter, and used his influence to see that the man obtained justice. But He was here on earth to do the greater thing: to bring to man the power of the Holy Spirit. And He would not lose the great aim in the smaller, as we are prone to do.

Miracles happened wherever Jesus went. But miracles do not happen in the churches of today—not often, not many, not unless a church is tremendously transfused with the Spirit of God. Most churches are dying of dry-rot, in the same way that Ananias and Sapphira died, only more slowly, more gradually. When church members break the eighth and ninth commandments (Exod. 20:15-16), as Ananias and Sapphira did, something in them dies, some spiritual vitality fades away. There is within their hearts the uneasiness of a secret guilt, and they are so uncomfortable about it that they either reason it away or try to forget it. Then it only goes deeper into the unconscious, and a door is closed between them and God, and a slow death begins within them.

When people break the seventh commandment (Exod. 20:14) and teach men so, as happens even in churches today, the Spirit of God is grieved, and no matter how much they rationize adultery, saying that it is really love, that it hurts nobody, and so forth, something deep within them loses its vitality, and a slow death begins in their spirits. They know with the heart what the conscious does not accept: that the adultery is sin against God. The spirit of a man and the spirit of a woman merge in the marriage act, making them one flesh, and this is God's plan. A man should become one flesh with his own wife and a woman with her husband. But the remainder of the love-power of their spirits they owe to God Himself, and not to illicit acts with other human beings. Why? Because sex is part of the flow of creativity which makes man a living soul. To squander it by fulfilling every wandering desire is to weaken one's creativity. It should, rather, be sublimated or transformed into that urge and zest of creative power that is man's most completely satisfactory joy. Therefore it is wise, as soon as one finds oneself falling in love with a person whom one cannot marry, to lift that feeling higher and to turn it into creative power. That is why Jesus placed such emphasis on the thoughts that lead to actions that are off the beam of spiritual power. (E.g., Matt. 5:28)

Similarly when a man nourishes within himself hate and anger, and refuses to forgive or be forgiven, he is taking the first step, as Jesus said, toward the final and terrible act of murder (Matt. 5:22), just as when a man indulges in brooding upon lust he is taking the first step toward adultery. Jesus did not say that the first step is as destructive as the last step. He did not say that one might as well kill somebody as to hate him because the first step is as bad as the last. He warned against even taking the first step, in His great horror that people might cut themselves off from God by going all the way into active, outbreaking sin.

"If all this is so," you may be thinking, "what man can stand before God?"

Why—any man can! That is the reason Jesus came and gave His life for us! Any man, if he wants to stand before God and be filled with His Spirit, can say, "Lord, I'm sorry! Please forgive me and help me not to sin any more," and can be reinstated in power and in love. The life of the Spirit will again flow through him. But if he will not say this—if he holds out against God—then a slow death begins in him.

We cannot lie unto God.

As Peter said to Ananias, "Why hath Satan filled thine heart to lie to the Holy Ghost, and to keep back part of the price of the land? Whiles it remained, was it not thine own? And after it was sold, was it not in thine own power?...Thou hast not lied unto men, but unto God." (Acts 5:3-4)

Some people today say, "God is dead!" In a sense it is true. God is dead inside of them. But in His world He is most terrifyingly alive!

However, when He is dead within us, we do not even know that He is alive anywhere. And without Him who is actually the very breath of our being, all the values of life grow dim and fade away. A lead article in *Esquire* magazine (July, 1968) gives an accurate and disheartening picture of this inner death, when the values of life fade out. What is the use of working from eight to five, says the author, and what does one gain? Nothing, is his answer. Poor dear, one gains life—but that is nothing to him. In the China of my childhood, man worked from the time the sun rose until it set, and gained a mud hut to house his family in, and a few grains of rice. If he were able to eat two meals a day, he considered himself a fortunate man. Life was good, because the very effort of working lends nobility to life, and makes rest sweet. A Chinese would squat in his doorway of an

evening, eat his rice from a bowl with wooden chop-
sticks, watch his little brown children play around him,
and be filled with deep content. He did not know God
as we know God, but he was a creator, working with his
hands the things that are good. Therefore he knew
creativity, and he knew it at the simple level of the
brown earth, rain, wind, and sunshine.

We of today are too far away from God, and too far
from the earth that God has made. And the most thera-
peutic and deeply comforting of all activities, simple
manual labor, we have denied to ourselves. We have
been convinced that we should all be equal, and that
every man should ride in a car, and spend the day sitting in an office. And someone has sold us women on
the idea that we should press a button or open a frozen
package for all that we need to eat, and spend the day
watching television. So we lose our hold on life and
creativity, and we lose our hold on God, whose laws are
too much trouble for us to keep.

If we can get God back into our souls, He will show
us also how to get back the joy of the earth, the pure
joy of living upon it and the delight of serving it.

But is it worth it: to keep God's laws so that the window of our souls will be open to Him? Is life worth it?
Because this is life and the secret of life. Is our world
worth it for the sake of our children, even if we ourselves are tired of life? Do we really like our world the
way it is? Are we content with negativism and despair?
Are was happy for our sons to be called away into a
war in which no one believes? Are we content that one
can no longer walk the streets, nor address a public
meeting, without danger of being shot? Are we pleased
that our daughters should bring forth illegitimate babies,
unless they are clever enough with their fornication to
avoid it? Do we really like this kind of world?

If we do not like it, then surely, before we jump off a
bridge, we may as well try to return to the Maker of the
world. He does not like it either, and He will make a
better world through us if we will but open the doors of
our souls to Him. The only hope of the world is this

kind of moral rearmament. We have tried everything else; we continually try everything else; and it continually fails.

We cannot keep the moral laws, however, if we try to do so all by ourselves, without the love and forgiveness of Jesus Christ and the upholding power of His Holy Spirit. For generations man has failed in keeping these laws, and what has he done about his failure? He has lowered his standards, inventing laws that are easier to encompass but that are of little avail to the Almighty. I cannot imagine Jesus wringing His hands in the heavens because some girl wears earrings or puts a bit of powder on her face. I am not even sure that He is upset if we go to a Communion without fasting. My young son once said to his father, "Dad, why do some Episcopalians feel they must go to the Communion Service fasting? Jesus didn't. The first Communion Service was after supper."

And my husband, a most delightful person, made reply, "Well, the thing is, Jesus wasn't an Episcopalian."

Yes, we invent other rules, and thus feel guiltless about evading the original ones.

There is also another way in which we evade the strict, simple but implacable rules for the life of the Spirit that God revealed to man by planting them deeply and irrevocably within his spirit. We become very excited about taking the mote out of our brother's eye, and are able complacently to forget the beam in our own eye. (Matt. 7:3-5) A perfect example of this is in the descendants of those who sailed the seas and brought home slaves for a southern market, sometimes purchasing them from their own chiefs, sometimes stealing them, often losing half of them upon the way. Instead of facing their inherited guilt—for the sins of the fathers do pass on to the children, who have to live out the fathers' unfinished business—they become agitated with hatred against their fathers' customers, and rush down south to tell them how to act. Then they are able to return with complacency, ignoring the fact that the plight of the lonely Negro in northern cities is often more pitiable than the plight of those abiding in little log cabins on the edge of a southern forest, with roses climbing over a rickety porch, and a cat asleep on the doorstep.

Alas, we do not become free in the spirit by shouting against other people's misdeeds, nor do we become free in the spirit by inventing a set of negatives that the Creator never said, while we fail to obey the essential laws of forgiveness, purity, and honesty.

But what do we gain if we obey God's laws? We gain the whole world! We then become endued with power, so that every ability and every opportunity submerged within us blossoms into life! Not only that, but we are then open channels for God's power to flow through into the world—and He knows what He wants to do with it if only we will give Him an opening. Remember the old story of Abraham! God could have saved Sodom and Gomorrah if there had been only ten righteous ones through whom His power could work. (Gen. 18:23ff.) These need not be the sons of God, the friends of God, as Abraham was—His conscious and active agents upon earth. These could simply be those armed with the righteousness of keeping His laws as well as they knew them.

Maybe you will become one of the friends of God, like Abraham (Jas. 2:23), one of the sons of God upon whom the whole creation waits. (Rom. 8:19) The theory that God loves everyone equally is both unbiblical and impractical. In His capacity as creator, yes, He sends His rain on the just and the unjust (Matt. 5:45), and His sun shines upon all. But in His capacity as Savior and friend, He loves His own with a passionate and special love. (E.g., John 11:5; 13:23; Mark 10:21) We are taught to love everyone with the good will of God, holding no resentment even against our enemies, but forgiving them. But we are never told that we should love everyone—wife, child, grocery boy, and mailman—with the same degree of love.

Yes, there are some people great in prayer and in power because they have made themselves so available to God's love that they conduct a tremendous channel of His passionate creativity into the world. These are called the sons of God (John 1:12) or the children of God, and it is through them and in no other way that at last peace shall be made upon the earth. (Matt. 5:9)

The making of this peace will take master-builders: those who so care for their Lord and for their fellow men that they are willing to undertake and to carry on the rigorous training for the life of the Spirit that will enable them to become the sons of God.

15
Windows to Heaven

✶

If certain ones of today can be called the hippies, the early Christians might be called the happies—or even the happy hippies! For there were certain resemblances to the young people of today who refuse to conform to this world, and who seek that ephemeral, beyond-reason state that they call love.

There was, however, one profound difference: the first Christians recognized the inevitable law of creativity. Paul expressed it thus: "If any would not work, neither should he eat." (2 Thess. 3:10) They had no overpaternal state to make it possible to eat without working, and in this they were blessed. For work is in the nature of God, the Worker, and therefore the useful employment of mind and hands keeps the channel open for Him. Idleness, as ancient proverbs have told us, opens the way for the enemy, who lies in wait for an empty mind, that he may come in and seduce it to its destruction.

Why were the early Christians so happy that outsiders thought they must be drunk? (Acts 2.13) They received an inflow of a new power and a new energy: yes. But this did not open to them an easy road to success or financial gain. Quite the contrary! It led them often to danger and even to death. It was so contrary to accepted beliefs and standards that it enraged those in authority both in the government and in the church of that day, called the synagogue. Or one might put it this way: the power of God released in the world stirred up the opposition of the devil. But in spite of torture and death, and the milder persecutions of being cast out of family and church, these people were happy. They loved everybody, and prayed even for those who persecuted them, seeing that these were themselves persecuted by the real enemy, the devil. Thus they carried on the work of the first One who hung upon a cross and prayed for His enemies. (Luke 23:34) Thus they laid down their lives to make a shining road that we may walk thereon.

But why were they so happy? They believed, certainly, that when they died they would go to heaven and be with Christ. But Christians of today believe the same. I remember my parents and other missionaries, of whom I wrote in *The Second Mrs. Wu.* They were just as sure of going to heaven as were the early Christians, and it was to them a comfort and a joy. But they did not walk in the early Christians' state of incomprehensible bliss.

Then what was it that so uplifted these early Christians? True, they were filled with power. But, as I have said, the power that brought healing to many others was just as apt to bring death to themselves, so that can hardly explain their joy.

Let us glance back to the beginning, that we may understand this matter. In the beginning, we are made double beings: of the dust of the earth, and of the breath of God. We are two bodies living together, the spiritual body interpenetrating the flesh. The physical body makes us aware of this planet, earth, on which for the moment we live. We see it, hear it, feel it, taste it, smell it. With our reason we learn to understand it. But eye cannot see, neither can the ear hear, neither can the hands touch, the spiritual world in which we also live: a world that exists outside of this earth, and before this earth, and after this earth.

The earth is three-dimensional. The other world is four-dimensional, and indeed many-dimensional. Just as it would be impossible to explain this three-dimensional world to some creature, a worm perhaps, who can see only on a straight line, so it is impossible to explain in the word-symbols of our language the world that exists in other dimensions. This can be made clear by mathematics, as Ouspensky has explained in his remarkable book *Many-Dimensional Space and the Spiritual World*.

When the Holy Spirit of God entered into the early Christians, their own spirits, their spiritual beings, came to life and they *knew* that other world, not through science but by firsthand knowing. They walked in the abounding joy of its tremendous creativity, a creativity that made all the everyday work of this world take on new glory and new life, so that even servants (or as we would say, slaves) did their work with joy, as unto the Lord. They lived in a flow of power that from time to time flooded over the laws of the flesh, doing miracles by the laws and power of the Spirit: miracles of healing, of resurrection, of release and protection, of guidance, and of the taking of the spiritual body right out of the physical body so that it could see those things that are invisible. (E.g., Acts 3:1-11, 9:36-42; 5:17ff.; 10:1ff.; 2 Cor. 12:1-4)

True, in the Old Testament this happened occasionally to certain prophets, but it was as apt to bring them anguish as joy, for they saw a power far away and unavailable save to one perhaps out of a whole nation. And they saw the consequent danger and destruction of a people who would not walk in the light of that power but preferred to walk in darkness. (Isa. 24:1-12; Jer. 20:7-18; 42:19-22) Jeremiah and Isaiah had no companionship in their holy seeing. But the early Christians had the companionship of the whole church, and more than this, they had the companionship of the Holy Spirit of Jesus Christ, who had entered the world veiled in flesh and had become a part of mankind. He was available to them at all times, and through Him the Father, the Creator, was available to them at all times.

We also say in words that He is with us at all times. Beneath our words there is too often emptiness, but there need not be this emptiness, for we too can walk in the larger awareness; we too can live in two worlds at once!

The early Christians opened their eyes upon a larger dimension, as a baby after birth opens its eyes upon a larger world than the womb, and gradually learns to see, and to understand the things that it sees. Some such rebirth happened all of a sudden in the early Christians when the Holy Spirit first came to them, a light from beyond shining on every one of them like flames of fire awakening the dormant light within them. The *possibility* of holding and radiating this light was already in them. We might say crudely that the fixture was already there, as the light fixtures can be in a house before the power is connected to them. But when Jesus entered mankind a mysterious change took place, so that the fixtures in man, which were dormant ("dead in sin"—see Rom. 8:10), or which were unscrewed from their sockets, were cleansed and screwed in, needing only to be connected with the power so that the light could shine in them.

When Jesus arose into the heavens taking mankind with Him, and the new merger of God and man took place, the power of the Holy Spirit was made available to enter into those fixtures. The light of the other world could shine into this world. This light, then, illumines everything both in this world and in the world that we call heaven, and that coexists with the world that we see. The glory of the other world illumines everything in this world. Our vision is mysteriously extended. True, the light varies, dimming off and on, as the sun dims off and on when clouds are scudding over the sky.

On days when I am in tune with the other world, everything in this world takes on new light, sometimes symbolically and sometimes literally. On the best days, I can see about the trees the light of creativity that shines continually, but unseen, in everything. Even on the worst days I can see little motes of light shining and dancing in the air. This is what I paint into my pictures, and people often say, "Your landscapes are so full of light!" Yes, I see them that way.

(You can learn to see this light too, if you care to do so. Focus your eyes upon the sky, and then focus them about three feet away from yourself upon what you think is emptiness, and like as not the emptiness will become filled with tiny specks of light dancing about like water-beetles on top of a lake! This light comes from you yourself, and illumines the world about you.)

On the best days I can look at a flower and it seems to speak to me. I do not hear words, but I feel some sort of communication between me and the flower. Not only that, but as I look at mountains towering above my house there is also a sort of communication between us. At times I feel their unrest, as the uneasy earth shifts and moves miles below them, and I send to them the love and power of the Creator, comforting them in their continuing struggle to give birth to a planet. At other times I seem to feel them resting within the comfort of God's love, and peace flows from them to me as it did to David long ago when he wrote: "I will lift up mine eyes unto the hills, from whence cometh my help." (Ps. 121:1)

Now, a solemn, earthbound theologian reading this book might boggle here, and I don't blame him! He is one who tries to analyze the light of God, as a scientist might try to analyze electricity, and to put down into mathematical formulae exactly what it is. I am only a simple person who turns on the electricity and walks in its light. I know very well that my reason cannot understand these floods of inspired imagination, and I do not care, for I do not live by reason but by another sense above, below, and beyond reason.

Most of all, this light of the other world illumines people. I look upon them and see beyond the visible person to the real person. I see the locked-up powers, the unused possibilities within the person. I see who he really is. Thus I can listen quite calmly while he confesses the most grievous sins and the most shocking aberrations and perversions, and I can say, "Yes, but that is not your real self." I can ask God for a picture of his real self, and can see it and pass it on to him, and we can pray together that it will come to pass—that the person he originally is will be born upon this earth.

How does one acquire this power of holy seeing? One does not learn it, really. It is a gift of the Holy Spirit: the gift of the discernment of spirits, both those in the flesh and those not in the flesh. But one can prepare oneself to receive this gift by quieting the thinking of one's mind, and stilling one's tongue, and sinking one's awareness into the other person: by striving with all one's concentration to see beneath the surface to the reality of the spiritual being entombed, and perhaps tormented, in the flesh.

We live in the day when the Holy Spirit is being poured out upon all flesh, according to the promise of the Bible. (Joel 2:28) In this we can rejoice greatly, and in spite of all the troubles and dangers of our age we can lift up our heads, for our redemption draweth nigh. (Luke 21:28) But it is sad that so many who call themselves "spirit-filled" are not really filled. They are touched by the Holy Spirit, and they have spoken, and one hopes continue to speak, in tongues, to the great release of the spirit within them. But they are too easily contented. There is so much more that they can have: gifts of wisdom and knowledge, of faith and the doing of miracles; the real, apostolic gift of healing such as Peter had; the gifts of discernment and prophecy—so much more. And the world in its desperation needs all these gifts. Indeed, those of us who are in the world need above all to see beyond the discord of this earth into the reality of life's other dimensions.

How shall we do this? In what way does God reveal to us the glories of a world that cannot be described in three-dimensional words, because it is a many-dimensional world?

He shows us these realities of another life by a quickening of the spiritual vision, so that one sees with the other kind of seeing that some call the "third eye." This goes far beyond mere clairvoyance. Clairvoyance is a bit of a psychic gift of seeing things just beyond the range of physical vision. I do not claim to understand this gift, which is very far removed from my own quite earthy personality.

The seeing of visions, on the other hand, is a direct gift from God to man and can come to any Christian through his God-mediator, Jesus Christ. The Bible is full of these visions, sometimes for the purpose of guidance upon this earth (E.g., Matt. 1:20; 2:13; 2:19-20), and sometimes for the revealing of that other state of existence in which we are already living and which we call heaven. (Rev. 1:10-11; 4:1ff.; 19:1-6) To many people they come spontaneously, but others such as myself are too earthy for this, and visions do not come unless we open our awareness to receive them.

I do this in a very simple way. In my meditation time and place, I imagine myself wading out into the ocean and floating upon the waves, farther and farther out. It is a lovely feeling: the spray cold upon my face and the sun warm and tingling, the great waters upholding me and swinging me in their troughs like a baby in a cradle! Then I imagine my spiritual body, as a shape of light, arising out of my physical body and going higher and higher into the air. In so doing, I attach my consciousness to this spiritual body. True, I know where I am, and am not unaware of earthly reality. But also I can see from far above that physical body like a tiny doll floating upon the waves, while I go high, and higher—through a little cloud that bumps a bit as I enter it, and is cold and moist upon my face —higher yet, till the air is thin, and the sky is almost black, and one can see the stars although it is daylight —higher yet—and then I say, "Now Lord, this is as far as I can go. Open my eyes and show me what you want me to see."

Shall I tell you all that I have seen? Oh no! Go and see for yourself!

But this I will say: the pictures in which I walk (for

I seem to be actually there) are much like those of St. John on Patmos (Rev. 1:9), and even perhaps of David in the Twenty-third Psalm. Who knows whether David's green pastures and still waters were on earth or in an above-earth state of living? I know that my pictures of heaven are not literal. They are an attempt of the mind to put into recognizable symbols realities that cannot be quite expressed or described in any kind of symbol, either of words or of pictures, for they exist in many dimensions. Nevertheless, they express a reality for which the soul longs with great longing. Thus they feed one with new life and joy in the midst of a disturbing world.

I can feel my readers thinking, "What *is* she talking about?" Things like this: the gates of pearl (Rev. 21:21) look like great pearls, for they are luminous with the soft and gentle quality of light that one sees in a pearl. (They existed before there were any pearls, of course. Maybe the Creator thought it would be fun to make a tiny thing like them and hide it in the most unlikely place possible!) The gates of pearl do not have an opening in them. One goes directly through this gentle light, which apparently has a cleansing action, a change in the rate of vibration, to free us from earth and begin to fit us for the other kind of life.

The city is described as foursquare (Rev. 21:16), with three gates upon each side. Could this have any connection with the four main types of humanity recognized by psychologists, and variations within each type? Do we enter through the transforming pearly mist that our own being requires? I do not know. I am not trying to teach anything, only to communicate the idea that we are not limited to this earth: we have already passed from death unto life (John 5:24), and even now our spirits have access to the heavens. We do not need the dangerous way of drugs to take a trip! We can go on the wings of our own spirits. Neither do we need the yoga or kahuna type of training in meditation, though this would be preferable to drugs. (The Chinese have used opium for this purpose for thousands of years;

it has not increased their efficiency as human beings upon this earth.) Through Jesus Christ we have this power of ascending into another state of existence. St. Paul felt this so strongly that he said that the "old man" was dead because of sin (Rom. 6:6; 8:10ff.; Eph. 4:22; Col. 3:9); the person that he used to be was no more. But the new man was life through the power of the Holy Spirit of Jesus Christ. The new man was not alive but was a life-giver and the very principle of life!

Once when I was apparently within the Holy City in a vision or in the spirit, I asked the angel who was the only living being that I saw, "Why do I not see any people on these golden streets?" (Rev. 21:21) (The streets did appear like gold in my vision, but they were not hard and solid. Walking upon them was like walking in a shining golden dust, which of course was not really dust but one of the many radiations of light.) "I am sure there must be people here," I said to him. (One uses the masculine pronoun for an angel, and yet he was neither male nor female, neither human nor ghostly, but fluid and shining and very beautiful.) "Because it feels warm and friendly, but I don't see anyone."

"That is because," he said, not in words but in thought, "they have not yet received their resurrection bodies, and since you are still in a body, you are not allowed to see them. This is for your protection."

Mystery beyond mystery! There were living spiritual beings within the city, but in some way they had not yet reached the perfected state of their being. We state in the Creed that we believe in "the resurrection of the dead," or "the resurrection of the body," but we do not, and perhaps cannot, know what it means. We say, believe, feel, and know that our loved ones who loved Jesus while on this earth are alive and safe with Him in the other life. (John 14:2-3) Yet we say that we believe they will be resurrected, and perhaps we have a vague picture of them rising up among the lilies on their graves—at least, this is the way that many of us envision the resurrection, and who can blame us? For in the midst of a three-dimensional world we are trying to explain matters of the four-dimensional, and five-dimensional, and many-dimensional world of eternity. I have no idea what God does with the actual atoms that make up this physical body that I now inhabit. But apparently we are composite beings, both physical and spiritual, and without the physical, while most definitely alive and safe in the Lord, we are not completed. Some day we shall be made complete, and we shall have a new body. Jesus showed us what that new body would be like, for we are told that when He appears we shall be like Him. (1 John 3:2)

Many people, feeling the reality of this, know no other way to envision it except by the theory of reincarnation: that we shall again be put into a body of flesh upon this earth. I do hope not; that would be so dull! If we need an earth to live upon when we achieve our resurrection bodies, I think it would be more fun to at least try another planet. What are the "many mansions" that Jesus spoke of in His Father's house? (John 14:2) What are the various heavens mentioned: the "third heaven" (2 Cor. 12:2), the "first heaven" and a "new heaven" (Rev. 21:1), and so forth? I do not know. But God must have made this vast, teeming universe for some purpose that we cannot dream or imagine!

Why am I saying all this? To stimulate your imagination! Someone has said that anything that man is capable of imagining is, or may become, true. I do not know whether that is so, but certainly some things that man has imagined have become true. The necessity of this release of the spirit of man in dreaming and in imagining is seen in the persistent fairy stories and myths that have followed man through history, and that still follow. Our science fiction of today is a higher and wilder imagining than Hans Christian Andersen ever dreamed about!

Man cannot live by his reason alone, for his reason is only a part of his total awareness. He knows not only with his brain and its reasoning processes, but he knows also with his heart and its subterranean moods and sensations that do not depend on reason. He knows also with his spirit, or supermind, or the third eye within him, which sees beyond the bounds of human seeing.

As the great prophets of the New Testament opened their eyes and saw, they beheld not only coexisting states of life, but also from time to time glimpsed through the window of their spiritual eyes things that were to happen in the future, both upon this earth and in the heavens. This phenomenon of prophecy—kin, as it were, to that flash-in-the-pan sight that we call clairvoyance—took place indeed throughout the whole Bible, in dreams, in visions, and in direct contact. But it reached its climax in the final book of the Bible. For as the first book looked back with amazing accuracy to the far past, so the final book of the Bible looks forward to the future and the far future, even to what St. John calls "the end." (Rev. 2:26)

The past has happened; it is fixed. So the thumb-nail sketch of it quaintly presented in the book of Genesis may require a bit of interpretation, but its meaning becomes for the most part clear.

The future, however, is in the making. It is fluid and malleable. It has not yet happened. Part of its making even depends a bit on us, which is very disconcerting. Certain ones of us are to reign with Him upon the earth in the millennium. (Rev. 5:10) We are to fight with Him in the battle of Armageddon (Rev. 16:16), as we have promised to fight this spiritual warfare under His banner. We are to "watch and pray." (Mark 13:33) That is, we are to watch, we are to be cognizant and aware of the sweep and flow of events. We are also to pray concerning these events. For what? For protection, for the turning away of the "fate" of destruction, and finally for His will to be done on earth as it is in heaven. (Matt. 6:10) The pattern of His will in heaven is also told us in Revelation, Chapter 21. Note particularly verse 4: "And there shall be no more death, neither sorrow, nor crying, neither shall there be any more pain: for the former things are passed away." We are to believe that this shall come to pass. We are strictly ordered in the Lord's Prayer to pray "Thy kingdom come" and to end the prayer with "Amen," "So be it," "It shall be so."

Presumably, in His omniscience, God knows beforehand all that will be, but in giving us free will, He depends upon us to help Him sway the course of the future. We have a stake in the future.

I don't know whether all of you should even read the book of Revelation, for it can be very confusing and upsetting. Yet when I was a child this was my favorite book of the whole Bible. It contained, as it still contains, a healing and a comforting power greater than any in the Bible. Revelation spoke apparently not so much to my reason, as a child, as to my heart or my spirit. It created, or perhaps brought back to life, in me such an awareness of the reality of heaven that from that time to this hymns such as "Jerusalem the Golden" awake in me a sort of nostalgia unlike any other feeling that I have known.

If you read Revelation with understanding, it will awaken unknown healing powers within your spirit. But you will also find dismaying and horrible concepts that must have come to St. John in nightmares! Now maybe in these dreams, or visions, or nightmares, he saw into our very day, and had no words in which to translate what he saw, but could only use symbols. If he glimpsed jet planes throwing bombs upon the earth and setting fires to cities, how could he describe them except as dragons or horsemen raining death and destruction upon the earth? If he saw napalm bombs or gas warfare releasing a slow and creeping death, how could he describe it save as plagues, or the pale horse of death itself? (Rev. 6:8) No wonder that all this filled him with horror, and that he said that if it went on, there would be no life left upon the earth. And so there will not. We know only too well today that if someone presses the wrong button, atomic energy could wipe out all life.

Some say that St. John wrote in code, and that the

early Christians had an interpretation of these visions
and prophecies. This I do not know, nor do I feel it
my duty to search the Bible for pictures of doom, because we tend to draw toward ourselves the pictures
upon which our minds dwell. There may be those who
are called to focus their attention upon threats of punishment and destruction, in order to bring people to
repentance. But callings differ. I have brought many
people to repentance through focusing, instead, upon
the power of God's love. So, while I have often read
the whole book of Revelation, I frankly confess that I
study, memorize, and make my own the prophecies of
the coming of the kingdom of heaven rather than the
prophecies of doom. For I search the Scriptures in
order to find life and healing, not to find death. Jesus
said that He came to give life, and that more abundantly (John 10:10), and for that life I seek, in Revelation
as in the whole Bible.

I do not know how much of the warfare, destruction,
and death prophesied has already been fulfilled, and
how much remains to be fulfilled. But when I tend to
become frightened about it, I remember the words of
Jesus: "And when these things begin to come to pass,
then look up, and lift up your heads; for your redemption draweth nigh." (Luke 21:28)

However, as I search the book of Revelation looking for healing and comfort, certain problems stand in
my way. First, how can there be contradictory prophecies, as there most certainly are? And second, why do
some of these prophecies, as interpreted by the faithful, fail to come to pass? We have heard of truly good
Christians who work out the time of the return of the
Lord, and expect that on a certain day they will see
Him coming in the clouds, and that they will be
caught up and be with Him in the air. (1 Thess. 4:17)
I heard of one old lady who made, as did many others,
a white "ascension robe" against this Day of the Lord,
and had the forethought to put a drawstring around the
hem, so that she would go up decently and in order!
How we may laugh at such deluded people—for the

predicted day comes, and nothing happens—but we may also weep. If a dream is given, shall there be no interpretation of the dream? Or if a prophecy be given, and if good and faithful Christians try to understand the prophecy, will not the Lord help them to understand it aright?

I heard a speaker harangue for two hours about an earthquake prophesied for June, 1968, when Los Angeles and its environs would be totally destroyed. It did not come. Why? Can it be that some of the faithful—the "watchers"—felt the tension of the earth, knew the danger, and prayed as Abraham prayed for Sodom and Gomorrah? And can it be that more than ten "righteous" were found, so that the healing power of God could through them ease the tension of the San Andreas fault?

There is at least the possibility that prayer may be the factor that the prophets, both religious and scientific, have not taken into account. For many well-known seers have made such prophecies. Some of their prophesied catastrophes have happened, much as they saw them through the "third eye," their window to the future. But others have not happened. Why? Is the window not clear? Perhaps not.

St. Paul said that we "see through a glass, darkly." Our windows of the soul are not clear and open windows such as the one I look through now, watching the maple leaves dance in the sunshine against a background of dark pines. Our windows may be of oiled paper, as it were, like windows in old houses in China, so that we see vaguely the shapes of things, but can easily misinterpret those shapes. Or our windows may perhaps be more accurately called binoculars or telescopes, whose accurate seeing depends largely on their adjustment to our own eyes. We look down the tunnel of time and catch glimpses of things that shall be. But there are two variable factors.

First, as I have pointed out, those events are fluid and may be prevented, minimized, or postponed by praying as Jesus commanded, that God's will be done on earth as it is in heaven. (Matt. 6:10) If His will in heaven is that there shall be no more death, as we have just read in Revelation 21:4, surely it is within His will for us to pray that people be saved from destruction.

The second variable factor is that while we may "see" with the eyes of the spirit the coming of events, we may find it more difficult to judge the time of each event, to get correct perspective. Even in this three-dimensional world we need constantly to adjust to perspective. Much of our adjusting has become habitual. We have learned, for instance, that while a road seems to grow smaller in the distance, it is really the same width. But occasionally even on this earth we misjudge distances. When I was at Lone Pine, between desert and mountains, I saw what I thought was Mount Whitney, snow-crowned, rising high into the glittering blue sky. But someone told me that I was not really seeing Mount Whitney but a nearer peak, and that the one farther away which looked much smaller was actually Mount Whitney, the greatest peak of the Cascades.

Surely it is possible that an earthly prophet may see a peak of the future, but may not be able to adjust to the perspective of eternity. Jesus was the greatest among prophets, and yet He Himself said that He did not know the time of His final coming, nor did any man know it. (Mark 13:32)

Then what about all the lists of numbers in the book of Revelation: the days, months, and years? I know only that time in the spiritual kingdom is not the same as time upon this earth. In reading Revelation we are dealing not only with earth, bound to the standard of twenty-four hours in a day, and three hundred sixty-five days in a year, but we are dealing with the heavens, where there is no day or night, and maybe also with "many mansions," or many heavens, or many planets, whose time span is entirely different from ours. Perhaps, indeed, the lists and numbers of this book (E.g., Rev. 7:4-8; 9:15-21; 11:13; 14:3; 17:9-18; etc.) were a kind of code that the early Christians understood and we do not.

Now let us leave the question of numerology, which concerns most of us but little, and go to that other question with which we are most truly and terrifyingly concerned: Where are we going? What is the end of it all? Here we are on this swiftly whirling planet, and some of us would like to say, in the words of the Broadway play, "Stop the world. I want to get off." But we cannot stop the world in its swing through time. Moreover, we learn not only from the Bible but from the visioning of our own spirits that we do not stop, nor do we get off, even at death, but the spark of life of the spirit that is in us continues. How long, oh Lord, how long? Forever? Are we really immortal? And if we are, is that not a more terrifying thought even than death?

What then do the book of Revelation and other New Testament prophecies tell us about the end? How far do these windows on the future open the way for our visioning? And what shall the end be, according to the visions of the prophets?

There is an inconsistency about this subject. At one point we are told that the heavens shall be rolled up like a scroll and disappear (Rev. 6:14), and at another place St. Peter tells us that the earth shall be consumed with fervent heat. (2 Pet. 3:10) This is astronomically quite possible. Our earth depends for its light and life, and its pathway through the heavens, upon our sun, but even suns are not everlasting. God the Creator continues to create. There are new suns that shine with a bluish light. There are old suns that are dying, and their light dims a bit and becomes tinged with a reddish hue. Furthermore, not all suns die of old age, losing their life gradually. Occasionally a sun explodes and becomes for a few days a nova, a flaming inferno of burning gases at white heat, and then dies in ashes. Is our sun then destined to explode? Is that what St. Peter means when he says that not only the sun but the heavens— the air above this earth—shall be consumed with fervent heat and be no more? Or is this prophecy, and the others like it, one in which a prophet sees that which *may* be if we continue our blind race with death, exploding energies whose scope we ourselves do not understand?

The final two chapters of Revelation would seem to indicate that it is the latter. For here we are given a picture of a new heaven and new earth. (Rev. 21:1) This may be in the ethereal state of living that we call heaven, or it may be upon some other planet, or it may be here upon this transformed earth. Verses 2-4 of Chapter 21 seem to indicate a kingdom of heaven here upon this earth: "Behold, the tabernacle of God is with men, and he will dwell with them, and they shall be his people, and God himself shall be with them, and be their God. And God shall wipe away all tears from their eyes...."

Then an angel came to St. John and said, "Come hither, I will show thee the bride, the Lamb's wife." (Rev. 21:9) And continuing in this chapter we have a description of the Holy City, the new Jerusalem: that is, the new way of living, the new order of life, when God's will shall be done as it is in heaven. It is either a highly fanciful description, or highly meaningful, or both. "And he carried me away in the spirit to a great and high mountain, and showed me that great city, the holy Jerusalem, descending out of heaven from God, having the glory of God; and her light was like unto a stone most precious, even like a jasper stone, clear as crystal." (Rev. 21:10-11) And a few verses later: "And the city had no need of the sun, neither of the moon, to shine in it; for the glory of God did lighten it, and the Lamb is the light thereof." (Rev. 21:23)

The author is trying to describe a different kind of light: a light existing at a different radiation, light that is not light as we see it upon this earth, yet it is light, a kind of light so brilliant and "clear as crystal" that it cannot be seen with the human eye—a multidimensional light. Only the foundations of the walls—that is, on the outskirts, as it were—where this light breaks and merges with the ordinary light of the "nations of the world," as St. John describes it, are shining with many colors, like

those of many precious stones, as the light of the rainbow, where pure white light is broken up by the com-
bination of rain and sun, shines in the seven primary
colors. (Rev. 21:19-20) John is trying to describe a
thing that simply cannot be described in three-dimensional language upon a three-dimensional earth.

Is this "city" to be established here on this earth?
Revelation 21:24 sounds as though it might be. "And
the nations of them which are saved shall walk in the
light of it: and the kings of the earth do bring their
glory and honour unto it." But how can that be the
end state of this earth, as the book seems to picture it,
if the earth has already been destroyed, as other prophecies have so definitely indicated? Is the Holy City then
not on earth at all but in the heavens?

This would be rather an unsatisfactory end—an end
that is not an end. For in Revelation 21:27 we read:
"And there shall in no wise enter into it anything that
defileth, neither whatsoever worketh abomination, or
maketh a lie." In Revelation 21:8, John has already
said: "But the fearful, and unbelieving, and the abominable, and murderers, and whoremongers, and sorcerers,
and idolaters, and all liars, shall have their part in the
lake which burneth with fire and brimstone: which is
the second death."

If we are talking about a many-dimensional world, a
world in which there are no realities except spiritual
realities, then there is no actual fire and brimstone, any
more than there are actual jewels making up the foundations of the walls. In the latter case, St. John uses the
symbolism of jewels to try to describe a radiation of
light that is beyond our seeing. He is, by the same token,
using the symbolism of fire and brimstone to try to describe the anguish of a life in which there are no realities except spiritual realities. If one is burnt up with
lust and has no body through which to release it, then
what must be the inescapable torment of one's spirit?
If one is filled with anger and violence, and is in a state
of bodiless existence wherein it is impossible to express
that rage and violence, then what must be the torment

of frustration, and the deep and burning regret that one did not, while on earth, see the reality of life so as to prepare for it?

Is there no end to this torment? Is there no one who can save us from this second death? If all this is true, how could we be happy forever and forever, even though we ourselves enter the city and live in the light of it? For do we not care about the others who are still without? And can we be satisfied to accept the conclusion of Revelation 22:11: "He which is filthy, let him be filthy still"? Or that of Revelation 22:15: "For without are dogs, and sorcerers, and whoremongers and murderers, and idolaters, and whosoever loveth and maketh a lie"?

My friends do not include many dogs and whoremongers, or so I hope. But the thought of all liars having their part in the lake of fire (Rev. 21:8) is a bit disconcerting, for few of us are totally honest with ourselves or with our fellowmen, and many love to make a lie: to present a false picture of themselves to the world, and to live by that lie. What then? Is this really the end, this division of people into good and bad, wherein the good enjoy life forever, and the bad are tormented forever by their inability to live in a spiritual world? Is this the best that God can do? Is this the upshot of the redemption of Jesus Christ, for which He gave His life? Are we forbidden even to pray for those we love who have gone on into another state of existence? Are we ordered to have no hope for them—no hope at all?

Is this the end?

Or is that other picture the end: the picture of the whole earth and sky destroyed in one burst of inconceivable fire? (2 Pet. 3:10) These two picture can hardly coexist.

There is yet a third picture, looking far away through a very powerful telescope. "And I beheld," wrote St. John, "and I heard the voice of many angels round about the throne and the beasts and the elders." (Who were they? Living creatures no doubt from other planets, living in other forms than ours. If you read science fiction, you may have seen something like them described!) "And the number of them was ten thousand times ten thousand, and thousands of thousands; saying with a loud voice, Worthy is the Lamb that was slain to receive power, and riches, and wisdom, and strength, and honour, and glory, and blessing. And every creature which is in heaven, and on the earth, and under the earth, and such as are in the sea, and all that are in them, heard I saying, Blessing, and honour, and glory, and power, be unto Him that sitteth upon the throne, and unto the Lamb forever and ever." (Rev. 5:11-13)

Every creature! Every living creature that could be in any conceivable place. Every one. And concerning this St. Paul wrote: "Then cometh the end, when He shall have delivered up the kingdom to God, even the Father; when He shall have put down all rule and all authority and power." (1 Cor. 15:24)

And what then? Shall the little spark of life that is in us merge with the great glory of God and cease to have individual life? If so, very well. After a few million or billion years of being myself, I think I might be a little tired of it and be glad to hand over!

Or do we continue to live and reign with Him in some inconceivable way and place within this inconceivable universe? I do not know. But I know this: nothing in this universe is immortal—not mountains that explode or wear away or disappear under the sea— not seas themselves that are, in the long reaches of time, burnt dry—not planets that grow cold and lose their life, or are burnt up like flies in the explosion of their suns. Nothing is forever except God and the redeemed spirit of mankind that shall be caught up into His being and there remain.